cured

cured

Handcrafted Charcuteria & More

Charles Wekselbaum

STERLING EPICURE
New York

STERLING EPICURE
New York

An Imprint of Sterling Publishing
1166 Avenue of the Americas
New York, NY 10036

ISBN 978-1-4549-1701-4

Distributed in Canada by Sterling Publishing Co., Inc.
℅ Canadian Manda Group, 664 Annette Street
Toronto, Ontario, Canada M6S 2C8
Distributed in the United Kingdom by GMC Distribution Services
Castle Place, 166 High Street, Lewes, East Sussex, England BN7 1XU
Distributed in Australia by Capricorn Link (Australia) Pty. Ltd.
P.O. Box 704, Windsor, NSW 2756, Australia

For information about custom editions, special sales, and premium
and corporate purchases, please contact Sterling Special Sales at 800-805-5489
or specialsales@sterlingpublishing.com.

Manufactured in China

2 4 6 8 10 9 7 5 3 1

www.sterlingpublishing.com

Cover Design by Chris Thompson
Interior Design by Philip Buchanan
Illustrations by Rita Carroll
Photography by Bill Milne

CONTENTS

WHOLE MUSCLE 108

SALT-CURED FRUITS AND VEGETABLES

FOREWORD

There's nothing quite like the classic combination of cheese and charcuterie. Savory and salty, fatty and rich, these two foodstuffs pair perfectly to create wonderful hors d'oeuvres or a savory main course. It is this classic pairing of meat and cheese which lead me to meeting my good friend Charles Wekselbaum.

I met Charles many years ago. I own and operate three small businesses, one of which is a cold storage warehouse. Charlie came to my warehouse soon after founding Charlito's Cocina, looking to store his charcuterie. Although my business focus is cheese, my warehouse does work with select non-cheese companies. From the beginning, I remember being impressed by Charlie's thoughtful, reserved demeanor. Sometimes you meet someone, and you just know that they are going to be successful. I could tell that Charles was hell-bent on making his family proud of him, just like me. My passion for cheese and Charles's passion for charcuterie seemed to go hand-in-hand, and our separate journeys into the food industry had many overlaps and similarities, always coming back to a love of great food.

Out of all of the fine foods one might develop a passion for, mine is cheese. I love cheese! I often say that my life is cheese (some might say my life stinks in a good way)! My family has been importing cheese for three generations (my grandfather was one of the first men to import cheese into the United States), and my father pioneered many of today's cheese legends. Yes, my cholesterol is high, but my desire to make my family proud is even higher.

To honor my legacy, I own and operate three small businesses, all cheese-related. The first is a warehouse called Larkin Cold Storage which serves as a United States logistics hub for many of the world's finest cheeses. The second is a cheese-importing company called Columbia Cheese that focuses on small production dairies from traditional cheese-making countries like Switzerland, Germany, and Italy. To foster a relationship from maker to monger, I created an event called The Cheesemonger Invitational, which is like the Olympics for cheesemongers.

I am hell-bent on making good food more accessible to the people. A concept that Charles and I agree upon is that of "food fear." Food fear is experienced by many, and is characterized by intimidation by food that is "too fancy." Many people feel self-conscious and insecure when describing what they are tasting, smelling, and feeling as they eat. They restrict their vocabulary to "this tastes good" or "I don't like this very much" out of fear of being wrong about a fancy meal or special cheese. They

might even be too intimidated to begin learning more about the worlds of cheese or dry-cured meat. In my opinion, eating is a sensory experience to be explored and discussed. Good food is all about connecting with yourself, the people you are with, and the world around you. Taste is an intensely personal experience. Everyone should feel welcomed to learn about and enjoy specialty foods.

In order to begin to learn about and love cured and preserved foods like charcuterie and cheese, an understanding of the history that lead to these modern delicacies can help to add to the majesty and wonder of these wonderful food products.

For thousands and thousands of years, humanity's relationship with food was immediate and wholly dependent on connecting with the outside world. Life was simple and straightforward, but it was not easy. Every day was spent preparing for the meals that would come later that day and for meals that would come many months in the future. Winters were long, and summers were hot. The elements were harsh. Days were spent hunting, fishing, and gathering.

The human diet consisted of whole, unprocessed foods, including fruits, vegetables, meat, seafood, dairy, and grains. Our use of fire in preparing food and our knowledge of fermentation were key elements that helped to distinguish us from other species. We figured out how to make bread, and how to tranform milk into butter, yogurt, and cheese. We mastered using salt in preserving food. Learning how to preserve proteins was a tipping point in the growth of human civilization.

During the 18th century, humans figured out how to master machines and energized an industrial revolution. Handmade goods and products were replaced by machine-made items, which could be produced cheaply on a massive scale. Rural agrarian villages gave rise to urban factory cities. Families disconnected from the land. When people tried to farm in the city, the results were filthy and dangerous.

The industrial revolution gave rise to our current era, the information age. Our connections are now based on how well we are connected to the Internet. Everything we need to know is at our fingertips. We have more free time than ever. In theory, we can survive with all the basic necessities and never leave our homes. Sometimes I think my digital footprint is larger than my physical footprint.

Our current relationship with food is dramatically different from the lifestyle of early civilizations. We have transformed from being a species which was intimately connected to the land and hyper-aware of the origin of each meal to a society that might not acknowledge the fact that individually wrapped cuts of meat actually come from animals! I often wonder whether our lost connection to food is in fact hurting ourselves and our planet. For example, did you know that the demand for palm oil (a key ingredient in processed supermarket foods) has caused massive deforestation, a proven cause of climate change? Many scientists agree that industrial farming only adds to our climate change crisis.

This is why I really like this book. It serves as an amazing way for you to reconnect with food, to travel back in time and discover how humans survived for thousands and thousands of years.

Learn how to cure, a foundation of man's original diet, and you will see salt in a whole new light. Salt is not just pepper's best friend, a permanent fixture on tables everywhere. Salt is the uncle of civilization. Salt helps the most perishable of foods last for a very long time. Learn how to cure, and connect with the world around you just like your great great-great-great-great grandfather did. Use this book and share what you learn. Learning and sharing are tools which will help you to reconnect with family and friends, and then to reconnect them with their food history. Maybe for civilization to survive and thrive we, as people, need a simple cure. Like reconnecting with our food.

Charles and I both believe in returning to our roots to better understand where our food comes from. We use mealtime as an opportunity to reconnect with friends, family, and the world around us. I hope that this book can help to convey that ideal, as it teaches about curing and cooking with hand-cured ingredients.

—**Adam Moskowitz**

INTRODUCTION

I was born and raised in New York City, one of the world's great melting pots, to a Cuban-born Father and a New York-born Mother. My father opened a hardware store in Manhattan shortly after he emigrated from his native Cuba, at the age of 28. The store evolved over the years into a legendary New York institution, the story of which could fill the pages of its own epic book.

The store was an amazing place, one in which over 20 countries were represented and even more languages were spoken among the shop's staff. It was, in many ways, a true reflection of my father's personality: unconventional, authentic, welcoming, and full of heart. My father was loved and revered at his shop, and this was never more apparent than in the early 2000s, when he was in need of a kidney transplant. Eighteen people who worked in the store, not including his family, volunteered to donate a kidney. At one point, the hospital complained that their medical staff didn't have enough time to test all of the potential donors! My mother saw to it that each and every volunteer was tested and that my father got the best possible match.

When my parents married in 1982, my mother joined the business. I came along in 1984, and as I grew up became more involved in the business. Our family home was right across the street from the shop, and our lives revolved around the business. The workday never ended for our family. When my parents came home for dinner, we talked about work. When we woke up in the morning, work was the subtle elephant in the room. Needless to say, this environment of intensity, entrepreneurship, and controlled chaos had a profound effect on me.

When I was a kid, my family had a loosely observed tradition of eating dinner in Chinatown on Sunday nights. Our dinners there were a far cry from what you might consider a "traditional" Americanized Chinese-food meal. We ate no sesame chicken, no duck sauce, no steamed vegetable dumplings. Our dinners included duck's feet, sea cucumber, jellyfish, fish-head soup, abalone, and roast duck with its head still attached. And, yes, there was pork. A lot of pork! These dinners are some of my earliest culinary memories, and definitely some of my most inspirational.

The principles of Chinese gastronomy have undoubtedly informed the work that I do today, and I hope these principles come across throughout the pages of this book. Those principles are: use of real, well-sourced ingredients; relentless attention to detail; confidence in your food; and the understanding that food is essential to well-being and should be given the highest value (even if it doesn't fetch the highest price), that it represents one's culture and one's self, and, that it should be approachable, garnering the utmost respect, without intimidation or snobbery. I hope that I have communicated that in this book and, as you journey through these pages, that you can keep these principles in mind.

My mother is an excellent cook, and she made certain that my sister and I were well versed in the culinary arts and the tools required to cook well—from the pots, pans, knives, and kitchen gadgets that she brought home from the store to a relentless attention to her (and our) culinary instincts. We were exposed to a wide variety of food in our home, from simmered tongue to elaborate stews, from the most perfectly roasted chicken you can imagine to simple breakfasts of matzo and eggs.

Fast forward to adulthood—for many years, I imagined that I would pursue a career in my father's business. I had thought tirelessly about the role I might adopt in the store, and, after working there for a few years after college, my future seemed to be playing out as planned. But as the saying goes, life is what happens when you're busy making plans. Through a series of unforeseen circumstances, by the year 2010 working in my father's business was no longer an option for me. At 26, I found myself at a crossroads. I was extremely anxious to make the best of my circumstances, but I had no idea how to proceed.

In trying to figure out what to do next, I found myself struggling to balance a variety of impulses, necessities, passions, and goals. The only constant was the knowledge that I wanted to run my own business. This was a value so strongly planted in me by my father that no matter how hard I fought it, the idea remained a priority for me. I found myself considering my passions and hobbies, and food became a focus for me. I developed a fierce interest in preindustrial methods of preservation; specifically, how a food item as highly perishable as raw meat could be preserved without refrigeration or freezing, even in the conditions in which it is most prone to spoilage, for months and years at a time.

At this time, I was working in a kitchen, and was sent to a storage area to retrieve additional ingredients. As I retrieved carrots and onions, I had my "ah-ha moment," a turning point in my life.

I imagined an oversized room full of meats curing, a clear and yet vague vision which was enough to provide me with a new direction and goal. I also knew, however, that this was a long-term goal and I was committed to the journey that was necessary to achieve my vision. As Steve Jobs eloquently stated, "You can't connect the dots looking forward. You can only connect the dots looking backward." Had my opportunity in my father's business played out as expected, I would not have been working in the kitchen that triggered my new vision for my future. Had that vision not occurred, I may not have had my "ah-ha" moment. Charlito's Cocina might not exist, and, my life would be very different.

Meanwhile, back at the apartment in Queens I was sharing with two friends at the time, I had retrofitted a 1991 brown Sanyo mini-fridge into a drying box. I had bresaola and a couple of salamis in there at the time. I decided to funnel my energy into getting my meat-curing business up and running, and on that day in late 2010, Charlito's Cocina was born. We made our first sale the following July.

After five years, thousands of pounds of salami, hundreds of trips, countless roadblocks, too many sleepless nights, and a few gray hairs, my journey continues. There are no words that can do justice to just how important, formative, and valuable the journey, with all its stops, twists, and turns, has been.

I hope you find yourself the following pages informative and helpful. Use the recipes and information as they appear or let them lead you to some other, seemingly unrelated place of inspiration or growth, as I was led that day the chef tasked me with getting onions and carrots. I would like to thank you for taking the time to read this, and engage in this book. Thank you and *salud*!

—**Charles Wekselbaum**

HOW TO USE THIS BOOK:

- Stock your kitchen with tools of the trade on pages 20–22.
- Build your own fermentation chamber by following instructions on pages 24–26.
- Select the highest-quality ingredients by referencing buyer's guides at the start of each section of the book
- Design a beautiful, themed charcuterie board using the instructions at the start of each section of the book.
- Make your own fresh sausage with recipes on pages 45–46. Then dry-cure it to make salami with recipes on pages 67–134.
- Any recipe labeled SAUSAGE will lead to fresh-sausage, perfect for eating directly or curing into salami.
- Any recipe labeled CURED will provide a dry-curing instructional.
- Any recipe labeled COOKED implements fresh salami or a dry-cured ingredient into a delicious, prepared dish.
- Complement COOKED recipes with the curated wine pairings.

TOOLS OF THE TRADE

When it comes to tools, less is more. A small collection of solid, versatile tools is invaluable in turning out great food. A little investment can go a long way.

Below is a list of tools that will prepare you to explore the recipes in this book. A few important staples will take you much further than a drawer full of fancy gadgets. The key is having tools that will last and that can be cared for and maintained over a long period of time.

2 Sharp Knives

A solid knife will maintain its integrity for years if you take proper care of it. It will change your life in the kitchen! A steel or carbon-steel blade can be sharpened and honed over and over again without losing its integrity. While it's wonderful to have a whole set of great knives, I would say that you can do most things with just two knives.

If you can only buy one knife, get a 6" chef's knife. It will give you the most versatility and the most bang for your buck. It is large enough to butcher meat, but not so big that you can't complete precise jobs with finesse.

That said, if you can invest in two, which I recommend, try the following: an 8" chef's knife and a 4" paring knife. These two knives are like the wide roller and the precise little paintbrush of knives. One covers a large surface area with relatively few strokes, while the other works well in tight places, where the big roller is too cumbersome.

A Solid Cutting Board

There are so many options when it comes to cutting boards. I happen to prefer a wooden chopping block because I like the way it feels, it won't damage your knife blade, and it can be maintained easily with gentle soap, water, and salt. Despite its perks, wood should not go into the dishwasher, a major downside for some chefs. If I had to pick other cutting board materials, I'd go with bamboo or plastic.

In addition to cleanliness, the most important consideration in buying a cutting board is to ensure that it will not damage your knife blade. Glass, ceramic, and other alternative materials can easily destroy a solid blade.

At Least Two Cast-Iron Skillets: One Small, One Large

Cast-iron cookware can be the most versatile, long-lasting, effective, and economical tool in a kitchen. It can go on the stovetop, the oven, or the grill. It is a deep fryer, a baking pan, a nonstick skillet for eggs, the most effective vehicle for searing, and so much more. With proper care, cast iron can last a lifetime.

TIP

IF YOU'RE REALLY INTO KITCHEN KNIVES, I'D HIGHLY RECOMMEND A GOOD, HEAVY, STEEL, CHINESE CLEAVER. FOR MANY CHINESE CHEFS, THIS IS THE ONLY KNIFE USED IN THE KITCHEN. WITH WELL-HONED SKILL, ONE CAN BUTCHER, SLICE, CARVE, DICE, CHOP, AND PLATE WITH THIS HIGHLY RESPECTED, REVERED, AND LEGENDARY WORKHORSE OF A KITCHEN TOOL.

A Couple of Stainless Steel Bowls

There's no bowl better than a lightweight, easily maneuverable stainless steel bowl. A bowl should be easy to handle, simple to clean, and durable. Stainless steel bowls are used widely in restaurants, come in a wide variety of sizes, and are inexpensive, especially if you buy them at a restaurant supply store.

Rubber Spatula

This will help to minimize your waste when you're getting every last bit of your food out of a bowl, pot, or pan.

Four Pots

You can get by in any kitchen with four sizes of pots: An 8" frying pan, a 12" sauté pan, a 2-quart saucepan, and an 8-quart (or larger) stockpot. I suggest these sizes because they can handle meals of most sizes. The smaller pots are perfect for sauces or for a quick meal for yourself, while all four in combination can feed a crowd.

A Slotted Spoon

A slotted spoon can be used for frying, and it's perfect for plating foods cooked in liquid. Dishes like braised meat are cooked in liquid, but the liquid is left behind when plating. The slotted spoon will be a cherished companion when making these types of dishes.

A Mesh Strainer

For rinsing and straining, a mesh strainer will make your life much easier. Available in many styles, a standard metal mesh will suit most needs. Supplement with cheesecloth to strain out especially small particles.

A Pyrex® Measuring Cup

A Pyrex measuring cup is versatile and durable. I can't overstate what a useful tool this is! As far as I'm concerned, it's the only measuring cup you need, and it has a small footprint when compared with its metal and plastic cousins.

A Ladle

I used to think ladles could only be used for serving soups until I began using them for measuring, stirring, and separating solids from liquids. This versatile tool might surprise you with its many uses.

A Spice Grinder

Spices are most pungent when they are freshly ground. To maximize a spice's flavor, buy it whole and grind it just before use.

A Potato Peeler

You can do so much more than just peel potatoes with this tool. It can serve as a mini-mandolin, slicing fruits and vegetables into paper-thin shavings. Use it for delicate dishes and for garnishes.

Tools for Dry-Curing

At Least Two Rectangular Dishes

These dishes are used to salt your meats. I like Pyrex because it is break-resistant and does not absorb or impart flavor, but any container with similar dimensions will do.

A Sausage Press

Make sure to avoid stuffers. (They use a drive mechanism, which will smear the meat and can be quite frustrating to work with). A press will simply press the meat into the casing without smearing and with less frustration.

A Mixer with a Paddle Attachment

A paddle attachment is my preferred tool for mixing spices quickly and easily.

A Meat Grinder

This tool is a wonderful help in preparing meats. In many sausage recipes, grind type is specified by grinder attachment size.

A Pricker

This tool pricks holes in sausage casings to remove any air pockets, which might lead to improper drying. Most prickers have multiple sharp spines mounted on an ergonomic handle. This specialized tool is nice to have, but any sharp, tapered substitute is suitable for poking through your sausage casing.

A Scale

Dry-curing meats is as much a scientific experiment as it is a culinary art. The more precise your measurements are, the more delicious (and safer) your salami will be. Any food scale is a great kitchen staple. I recommend one that can handle at least 11 pounds for salami making.

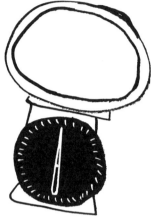

A Place for Hanging the Meats

Whether a rack, S-hooks, or a more complicated setup, your meats will need to hang with airflow on all sides for a number of weeks.

A Hygrometer

A hygrometer reads temperature and humidity. You can find them combined into one device, but they can also be purchased as two separate devices—one for measuring temperature and the other for measuring humidity. You can buy a hygrometer at many hardware stores, as well as through online retailers specializing in equipment for dry-curing.

Weights

Any tool that can be used to weigh down foods during salting serves our purposes. Cans, bricks wrapped in aluminum foil, and bacon presses are all easily accessible options.

Hotel Pan

I fill a hotel pan with salt water to introduce humidity into my fermentation/drying chamber. Any large bowl or container will do.

ALL ABOUT FERMENTATION

Fermentation is an important step in making dry-cured sausages. It serves as the acidification step in the process, the first of two steps to ensure a hostile environment for harmful bacteria. An acidic environment lowers the ability of harmful bacteria to grow, but it also makes it more difficult to pronounce flavors in your salami. The tangy flavor created by fermentation can be quite overpowering. Thus, getting the fermentation just right is a challenge, a balancing act, and a matter of personal preference.

The Importance of Acidity

Acidity is measured using the pH scale. The scale runs from 1 to 14, with 1 being the most acidic, 14 being the most nonacidic, or basic. Seven represents neutral acidity (mild dish soap has a pH around 7.5, lemon juice has a pH of 3). When a salami is first stuffed in the casing, its pH is generally between 5.6 and 5.9. The target pH after fermentation is 5.3. An inexpensive pH meter is a great tool to have for monitoring pH. Once you get below 5, the flavor of the product becomes significantly more tangy and acidic, which can mask or kill the flavors of the seasonings and spices in your salami. At 5.3, the environment is considered acidic enough to prevent the growth of harmful bacteria, but basic enough to preserve the flavors of the salami. That said, pH is a very important element to monitor. There is a great deal of nuance in getting it just right but, above all, it is an art that requires creativity, trial, and error.

FERMENTATION TEMPERATURE REFERENCE

TEMPERATURE	FAST OR SLOW	VERY MILD
70°-80°F	SLOW 72 HOURS OR MORE	VERY MILD MORE PRONOUNCED FLAVORS
79°-85°F	MEDIUM UP TO 72 HOURS	MILD TANG NICELY PRONOUNCED FLAVORS
86°F AND HIGHER	FAST UP TO 24 HOURS	HIGHLY TANGY/ACIDIC DISTINCTIVE "SALAMI" TANGINESS

MAKING A FERMENTATION AND/OR DRYING CHAMBER

Fermentation and drying chambers do not have to be complex or high-tech. They can be as simple as a box, a refrigerator, or even a small room or closet in your home. A standard oven can be used as a very effective fermentation or drying chamber with little preparation.

If you're willing to make an investment and you want something fancy, there are a number of luxurious products available for curing meats. That said, fermentation and drying rooms do not have to be fancy. On the following pages, you will find two methods for building a successful fermenting room. From there, you can obtain a variety of tools to help you hone your craft.

One reason fermenting within an enclosed space is preferable to working in a larger room is that it is easier to maintain a consistent environment in smaller spaces. When you first hang your salamis, especially if you fill the chamber, you'll see a significant spike in humidity because the sausages are wet, which will be very helpful to your fermentation. A small, enclosed closet in your house or basement will work well, too.

TIP

FERMENTATION AND DRYING ROOMS CAN EACH BE PUT TOGETHER IN THE SAME MANNER. BOTH SERVE THE SAME PURPOSE: THEY ARE ENCLOSURES THAT ALLOW YOU TO CONTROL TEMPERATURE AND HUMIDITY. FERMENTATION AND DRYING ROOMS CAN EVEN BE COMBINED IF YOU HAVE LIMITED SPACE. IF YOU'RE MAKING MORE THAN ONE BATCH DURING YOUR LONGER DRYING PERIOD, I RECOMMEND KEEPING THE SPACES SEPARATE.

Building a Modern Fermentation Chamber

What makes this method "modern" is an electrical plug! When I first began dry-curing, I used an old mini-fridge as my fermentation chamber. While it required some tweaking and tailoring, it got the job done. Here are my instructions for an entry-level fermentation chamber like the one I first used.

What You'll Need

- A refrigerator
- Nonbleach sanitizer and cleaning supplies (Places that sell home brew equipment usually have good options. White vinegar is also a good option.)
- A hygrometer
- A space heater
- A rod or hooks for hanging your salamis
- A hotel pan or mixing bowl
- A fan

NO NEED TO TURN THE REFRIGERATOR ON FOR FERMENTATION. THE REFRIGERATOR SERVES AS YOUR ENCLOSURE, BUT IF YOU TURN IT ON, IT WILL BECOME TOO COLD FOR THE FERMENTATION TO WORK PROPERLY. IF YOUR REFRIGERATOR DOOR DOESN'T CLOSE, THAT'S OK. SIMPLY COVER THE OPENING WITH A BLANKET, SHEET, OR TOWEL, TO HELP KEEP THE ENVIRONMENT INSIDE AS CONSISTENT AS POSSIBLE.

Instructions

1. Get your refrigerator. The amount of product you intend to make and your space will determine the size, but typically a standard fridge works well. If you plan on keeping the fermentation and drying chambers separate (which I recommend), bear in mind that the drying chamber should be bigger than the fermentation chamber because fermentation time is much shorter than drying times (fermentation typically takes no more than 72 hours, while drying could take up to 6 months or even longer).

2. Clean and sanitize the refrigerator very well, whether it's used or new. It has to be immaculate before you start. Let it air out with the door open, preferably with a fan blowing on the inside.

3. Clear as much space inside the fridge as you can, leaving one rack as high up as you can put it. This is the rack you will use to hang your meats.

4. Place the hygrometer on top of the rack.

5. Get the smallest space heater you can find and place it in the bottom of the refrigerator. It's OK to leave the door cracked if the heater or its power cord prevents the door from shutting entirely. Reference the guide to fermentation temperatures in the table on page 23. You might not need to use the heater if ambient temperature is high enough.

6. Place a hotel pan with well-salted water on the bottom of the refrigerator. The water will help you create humidity, which is very important for both fermentation and drying, while the salt will help keep the water from becoming a breeding ground for unwanted bacteria.

Building an Old-School Fermentation Chamber

Although this method takes a bit of elbow grease, the payoff is massive. With a little bit of time, some power tools, and easy-to-source materials, you have the benefit of a rustic, inexpensive, yet classic fermentation chamber for your salami.

What You'll Need

- A hammer

- A box of heavy-duty nails

- 5 square sheets of thick, untreated wood, no smaller than 5' x 5' (1.5m x 1.5m)

- 1" (2.5 cm) hole saw drill bit

- 9 untreated wooden dowels ¾" (2 cm) in diameter; make sure the dowels are 6" (15 cm) longer than the width of your box

- Heavy-duty curtain to tightly cover the entire opening

- Something to elevate the box (such as a pallet, bricks, concrete blocks, or the like; you can also build this on an elevated surface like a counter—the goal is to discourage any unwanted visitors)

- A heating element—you can use a space heater, but if you want to keep it old school, use bricks or cast-iron skillets that have been thoroughly heated in the fireplace or on the woodstove. These retain heat well and will create the heat in your drying room that's needed for the fermentation to work.

Instructions

1. Nail the boards together to make a box, using at least 3 nails per side. You will be left with 1 open side.

2. Drill 8 holes, evenly spaced, 6" (15 cm) from the top of your box on each side of the box. You will be drilling 32 holes in total. Make sure these holes are evenly spaced and are parallel to each other. This is where your dowels will go, which is where your salamis will hang. If the measurements aren't right, your products will be lopsided while they hang.

3. Make 2 more holes on each side of the box, as close to the top edge and to the front as you can get them. This is where your curtain will hang.

4. Clean out any dust or wood particles from the construction and the holes.

5. Insert the dowels into the holes. You will hang the salamis from these dowels.

6. Hang the curtain on the front dowel, covering the opening to the box.

TIP

IN TRADITIONALLY MADE DRY-CURED SAUSAGES, THERE IS NO FERMENTATION STEP AND NO CULTURES ARE USED. THE SALAMIS ARE LEFT IN ONE AREA TO DRY WHILE THE CLIMATE IS FALL-LIKE—COOL, BUT NOT COLD; MISTY, BUT NOT MUGGY. IN ORDER TO CONTROL BACTERIAL GROWTH, THE PEOPLE WHO MAKE AND EAT THESE SALAMIS RELY PRIMARILY ON WATER ACTIVITY, THEIR OWN STRONG IMMUNE SYSTEMS, AND HIGH-QUALITY MEAT. FOR THE ENVIRONMENT, THINK MORNINGS ON A MOUNTAIN IN OCTOBER. THE IDEA IS THAT, IN HIGH-QUALITY MEAT, THERE IS ENOUGH BENEFICIAL BACTERIA NATURALLY OCCURRING IN THE MEAT TO ENSURE PROPER ACIDIFICATION AND DRYING. THAT SAID, A DEDICATED FERMENTATION STEP WILL GIVE YOUR SALAMI A BETTER CHANCE OF CURING WELL.

FROM FARM TO KITCHEN

The Process of Making Salami

1. Raising animal

The animal is raised, preferably in a clean, open environment, with access to the outdoors. It eats a clean and natural diet and is ideally not administered any antibiotics, growth hormones, growth stimulants or promoters.

2. Sacrifice

The animal is sacrificed in as low stress a manner as possible. This includes, but is not limited to, orderly and smooth transport, ensuring that no other animals are present, performing the sacrifice quickly, so any pain the animal feels is kept to a minimum. The most "humane" way of doing this today by "stunning," which imposes instant unconsciousness unto the animal.

3. Butchering

Butchering can be done in a variety of ways. Styles of butchering consistently vary from country to country and region to region. The important information to remember when butchering for salami making, is to a) separate the lean meat from the hard fat and b) make sure it is trimmed of its nerves, tendons, and silver skin. While certain cuts are better for making salami than others, any cut can theoretically be used, as long as the meat and fat are properly separated and measured out.

4. Chopping/Grinding

This is where the coarseness of your salami gets determined. It also plays a vital role in how your lean and fat are visually defined in the finished salami. Lean and fat should be kept cold during this process, and handled minimally, to keep them from smearing, and to ensure that the lean and the fat maintain their definition as much as possible. It is important that the lean meat does not become covered in fat, which will prevent it from drying and can cause the salami to spoil.

CAMPO SECO AT THE BEGINNING OF THE FERMENTATION PROCESS (LESS THAN 2 HOURS OLD)

CAMPO SECO – 1 WEEK OLD (BEGINNING OF DRYING PROCESS)

CAMPO SECO – MID-AGING (ABOUT 2 WEEKS OLD)

5. Mixing

This is where salts, spices, and cultures get incorporated into the meat. The important thing to remember here is to mix only until the salt, spices, and cultures are just incorporated. Over mixing will warm the meat, and start to smear it, thus beginning to break down the proteins in the meats, which will affect the integrity of the salami.

6. Resting

This will give your meat a chance to relax and, as I like to think of it, "regain its composure," after the intense grinding and mixing process. It will also allow your spices to penetrate the meat thoroughly. This usually lasts one or two days.

7. Fermentation

This is the initial stage of curing and the first of the two main steps that make non-heat treated salami safe to eat. During fermentation, beneficial bacteria present in the meat will consume any sugars present in the mixture. The product of this "digestion" of sugars is a form of acid, which creates an acidic environment, inhospitable to harmful bacteria. Fermentation is usually completed in 5 days or less. Slightly warmer temperatures encourage microbial activity, which enables the fermentation. The fermentation step is the point at which the "tanginess" of the salami will begin to take shape. The warmer the fermentation environment is, the faster the fermentation will occur, and the tangier the salami will be. The tangier it becomes, the more difficult it is to discern the individual flavors of the various spices and components of your salami. For this reason, I prefer a slower fermentation, so we get some tanginess, but also the flavors of the meat, salt, and spices. Our target PH for the salami to reach during fermentation is between 5.1 and 5.3. Below 5.1 and the salami becomes too acidic for my taste. Above 5.3, and the environment is not acidic enough to prevent the growth of harmful bacteria.

8. Drying

The length of this period varies widely. The idea is to dry until it has achieved shelf stability, as well as allowing the flavor profile to mature to your taste. A good drying room should be kept at moderate temperature, with sufficient humidity. The environment should feel like a misty morning in Fall. If the environment is not right (i.e. too cold, too warm, or too dry), the salami will not dry properly. This period typically lasts as little as two weeks for a more moist, smaller salami, or up to 6 months for a drier, larger salami.

9. Slicing and serving

Slice it thin, slice it thick, slice it in between, cube it, slice it width-wise, slice it lengthwise. Just slice it how you like it! My favorite is lengthwise, in long and thin pieces. This is great if you have a slicer.

CAMPO SECO – 3 WEEKS OLD

CAMPO SECO – ALMOST DRY

BUILDING A
FANTASTIC
CHARCUTERIE
BOARD

There are so many variables in making a great charcuterie board. How many meats should you choose? What about cheeses, veggies, and accompaniments? Should you put bread on the plate or on the side? Should everything fit onto one large board or should each component have its own, smaller board? The truth is, there really isn't a wrong answer here. The opportunity to be creative is one of the best parts of assembling a charcuterie board! Because most of the components are prepared ahead of time, creating a charcuterie board is an exercise in the art of arrangement. Here are some tips to help you balance delicious flavor on your charcuterie board with visual and textural interest.

TIP

WHILE I PREFER SLICING BY HAND, AS IT'S DEFINITELY THE CLASSIC WAY, HAVING A SLICER CAN BE HANDY. SLICERS VARY IN PRICE FROM $100 TO OVER $5,000. WHILE THE CHEAPER ONES WORK, YOU CAN GET AN ENTRY-LEVEL PROFESSIONAL SLICER FOR AROUND $400, AND THE BENEFITS THAT BEGIN AT THIS PRICE POINT ARE IMMEASURABLE.

- **Keep it simple:** Don't overthink this! Great individual components will speak for themselves. Quality cured meats and great cheeses don't lie. Too many accoutrements can be a distraction.

- **Make it abundant:** Abundance is a sign of welcome. I know that these ingredients can be expensive, but it's so important to serve your guests in a way that lets them feel confident about partaking in the board without sacrificing someone else's share. Make sure that everyone can have at least a few bites.

- **Present at least three meats:** One way to think about this is to have at least one simple meat, one mild but spiced meat, and one spicy meat. Normally I like to have at least five meats on my boards.

- **Present at least three cheeses:** There are so many ways to go about this. You can choose one soft, one medium, and one hard cheese; or one cow, one goat, and one sheep cheese. Explore flavors and textures.

- **Vary the way you cut:** If you slice one salami into rounds, slice the others lengthwise or on a strong bias. With cheese, if you've sliced a hard cheese into triangles, try serving a soft cheese whole with a serving utensil on the board. Not only does this look beautiful, but it helps people differentiate between items on the board.

- **Present at least one sweet element:** At Charlito's Cocina, we created fruit "salamis" expressly for this purpose. In the absence of a fruit "salami," you can use dried fruit, preserves, or mostardas.

- **Don't skimp on the bread:** If you have access to really great bread, use it. Great bread will enhance everything on the board and make all the elements shine.

- **Warm the bread:** A cast-iron skillet is great for this. If you have a press to weigh down the bread, even better. If the bread isn't super-fresh and delicious, grilling or toasting will really turn it around. The warmth from the bread will open up the multitudes of flavors in a tasty salami.

- **Don't be afraid to serve whole-wheat or multigrain bread:** Aside from their health benefits, whole-wheat and multigrain breads add additional dimensions of flavor. Nutty, earthy, wholesome—these are all good things.

- **If you're feeling ambitious, use a variation on bread:** Gnocco frito (puffy fried mini-bread from Italy), chickpea flatbread, plantain chips, mini-popovers, and homemade crackers are all tasty ideas.

- **Incorporate one crunchy element if possible:** Toasted walnuts, homemade potato chips, or chicharrons are all great options.

- **Be careful to keep it from looking too manicured:** A slightly relaxed presentation makes the board seem more inviting. You might want to layer some slices of meat in one section of the board, and "pile" slices in a different section.

- **Know your crowd:** Are your guests comfortable gobbling down a ½" piece of salami without hesitation? If so, thickly hand-cut your meats! Don't be shy. Slicing thin isn't the only way. On the flip side, is it a leaner, more delicate crowd? Are you serving a plate for a fashion magazine gathering in Tribeca? If so, show off those thin slicing skills. Just make sure you have a very sharp knife.

- **Cut meats and cheeses as close to serving time as possible;** otherwise, they'll dry out. Keep soft cheeses whole and serve with a utensil for self-service. It's fine to serve all the cheeses like that if you prefer.

DRY-CURING WITH SALT: HOW DOES IT WORK?

When I was a teenager I found a recipe for braised, dry-rubbed pork belly. It sounded delicious so I decided I'd make it. The recipe called for a variety of spices, and instructed the home chef to coat the pork belly in dry-rub and leave it to sit in the refrigerator overnight. I wrapped the belly in plastic wrap and did as the recipe said. When I woke up the next day, I discovered a pool of meat juice from the belly covering the refrigerator shelf! I learned the hard way that salt draws out moisture.

I didn't realize at the time that the messy puddle of meat juice and soggy carton of eggs in my refrigerator were the result of an ancient preservation process that remains relevant through present day. As illustrated by my failed pork-belly experiment, salt is excellent at drawing out moisture, which happens to be one of two key elements which contribute to bacterial growth. If you can control the moisture and temperature of a food product, you have a great chance of successfully preserving that food.

Salt has the additional benefit of creating an especially inhospitable environment for bacteria. Perhaps it was this multitude of benefits that led salt to be celebrated by the Romans as so valuable that the latin word for salt, "Sal," provides the root of the modern English word "Salary."

Here's how salt preservation works:

1. Salt is applied to a food product.

2. As the salt penetrates the food, moisture is drawn out.

3. Salt creates a hostile environment for bacteria to grow.

4. Once moisture is reduced to a low enough level, bacteria cannot grow, as there is no moisture for it to feed off of.

SPICED SALTS

A Most Versatile Salt: Four-Spice

YIELD: 6 cups (1.4 l)

This derives from a classic French spice blend, called "Quatre épices."
Use it in lieu of straight salt to add some zest to meats, veggies, and starches.

INGREDIENTS

- 4 CUPS (946 ML) SEA SALT
- 1/2 CUP (118 ML) NUTMEG
- 1/2 CUP (118 ML) CLOVES
- 1/2 CUP (118 ML) FINELY CHOPPED GINGER
- 1/2 CUP (118 ML) PEPPER (IF YOU'RE NOT CRAZY ABOUT PEPPER, YOU CAN SUBSTITUTE AN ADDITIONAL 1/2 CUP [118 ML] GINGER IN LIEU OF PEPPER)

SPECIAL TOOLS

- LARGE MIXING BOWL
- LARGE MASON JAR

INSTRUCTIONS

1. PUT ALL THE INGREDIENTS IN A LARGE MIXING BOWL, MIXING ALL THE INGREDIENTS UNTIL THEY'RE WELL-COMBINED.

2. MOVE TO A JAR FOR STORAGE. STORE INDEFINITELY.

A Spicy Salt: Chilies in Salt

YIELD: 4 cups (946 ml)

Lend an instant kick to your table by using this chili-laden seasoning in lieu of standard table salt. I love to use this spicy salt in chorizo and eggs to liven up my morning meal.

INGREDIENTS

- 1/2 CUP (118 ML) WHOLE PIQUIN CHILIS
- 1/2 CUP (118 ML) WHOLE CHILI DEL ARBOL
- 3 CUPS (710 ML) SALT

SPECIAL TOOLS

- CHEF'S KNIFE
- LARGE MIXING BOWL
- MASON JAR

INSTRUCTIONS

1. GENTLY CRUSH PIQUIN CHILIS USING A CHEF'S KNIFE, BEING CAREFUL NOT TO CUT THE PIQUIN CHILIS INTO PIECES.

2. CUT THE ARBOL CHILIS IN HALF.

3. PUT ALL THE INGREDIENTS INTO A LARGE MIXING BOWL, MIXING ALL THE INGREDIENTS UNTIL THEY'RE WELL-COMBINED. MOVE TO A JAR FOR STORAGE. THE LONGER YOU LET THE MIXTURE SIT, THE SPICIER IT WILL BECOME. LET THE MIXTURE SIT FOR AT LEAST 2 DAYS BEFORE USE.

4. STORE INDEFINITELY.

Dried Rosemary in Salt

YIELD: 2½ cups (591 ml)

I made this salt blend for the first time after purchasing a bundle of fresh rosemary, and cooking with only a few sprigs. When cleaning out my refrigerator a few days later, I decided to give the herb new life by infusing some salt. This technique works with many different leftover herbs, so don't be scared to experiment!

INGREDIENTS

- 8 SPRINGS OF FRESH ROSEMARY
- 2 CUPS (473 ML) SEA SALT

SPECIAL TOOLS

- MASON JAR

INSTRUCTIONS

1. SEPARATE THE ROSEMARY LEAVES FROM THE SPRIGS. ROUGHLY CHOP THE LEAVES IF A SMOOTHER TEXTURE IS DESIRED.

2. PLACE THE CHOPPED ROSEMARY LEAVES AND THE SALT IN A LARGE MIXING BOWL, INCORPORATING INGREDIENTS UNTIL WELL-COMBINED.

3. MOVE TO A MASON JAR FOR STORAGE. STORE INDEFINITELY.

Three-Herb Salt

YIELD: 2 cups (473 ml)

Here's a great way to use leftover herbs. Think of the quantities in this recipe as guidelines: You can throw in whatever amounts you have on hand. The beauty of this salt is that you're taking a bunch of herbs that would otherwise go to waste and creating a seasoning that is aromatic, versatile, and incredibly useful for cooking and curing.

INGREDIENTS

- 20 SAGE LEAVES
- 15 SPRIGS THYME
- 5 SPRIGS ROSEMARY
- 2 CUPS (473 ML) SALT

SPECIAL TOOLS

- LARGE MIXING BOWL
- LARGE MASON JAR

INSTRUCTIONS

1. REMOVE ALL HERB LEAVES FROM THEIR STEMS.

2. COMBINE ALL THE HERBS AND CHOP COARSELY.

3. PUT ALL THE INGREDIENTS INTO A LARGE MIXING BOWL, MIXING THE INGREDIENTS UNTIL WELL-COMBINED.

4. MOVE TO A MASON JAR FOR STORAGE. STORE INDEFINITELY.

Garlic, Juniper Berry, and Rosemary Salt

YIELD: 3 cups (710 ml)

Another iteration of infused salt, this seasoning includes juniper berries. This citrusy, slightly piney ingredient goes well with meats and promises to delight diners with its mysterious flavor profile.

INGREDIENTS

- 10 CLOVES GARLIC
- 7 SPRIGS ROSEMARY
- 1/2 CUP (118 ML) JUNIPER BERRIES
- 2 CUPS (473 ML) SALT

SPECIAL TOOLS

- LARGE MIXING BOWL
- MASON JAR

INSTRUCTIONS

1. ROUGHLY CHOP THE GARLIC.

2. SEPARATE ROSEMARY LEAVES FROM SPRIGS AND ROUGHLY CHOP.

3. PUT ALL THE INGREDIENTS IN A LARGE MIXING BOWL, MIXING THE INGREDIENTS UNTIL WELL-COMBINED. MOVE TO A MASON JAR FOR STORAGE.

4. STORE INDEFINITELY.

Five-Spice Salt (with Six Spices) — YIELD: 6⅓ cups (1.5 l ml)

This one is a classic Asian spice. It's one of my favorites, and I love incorporating it into sausages. A little chopped meat with some five-spice salt will take you a long way.

INGREDIENTS

- 3/4 CUP (177 ML) FINELY CHOPPED GINGER
- 1/2 CUP (118 ML) STAR ANISE POWDER
- 1/2 CUP (118 ML) SICHUAN PEPPER, GROUND (YOU CAN BUY THIS GROUND, BUT IF YOU'RE ABLE TO BUY IT WHOLE AND GRIND IT FRESH AT HOME IN A SPICE/COFFEE GRINDER, THAT'S THE WAY TO GO)
- 1/2 CUP (118 ML) CLOVES, POWDERED
- 1/4 CUP (59 ML) GALANGAL POWDER (A GINGER RELATIVE)
- 1/3 CUP (78 ML) CINNAMON, POWDERED
- 4 CUPS (946 ML) SALT

SPECIAL TOOLS

- LARGE MIXING BOWL
- LARGE MASON JAR

INSTRUCTIONS

1. PUT ALL INGREDIENTS IN A LARGE MIXING BOWL, MIXING UNTIL WELL-COMBINED.
2. MOVE TO A MASON JAR FOR STORAGE. STORE INDEFINITELY.

SAUSAGE & SALAMI

RENDERED-CHORIZO FAT

CERVEZA SECA

SALAMI PICANTE

COUNTRY SALAMI

CHORIZO

THE ULTIMATE CHARCUTERIE BOARD

I consider this to be the ultimate, classic charcuterie board. It works well as a "nibbler" plate for friends and family, although I have been known to make one for myself when the urge has arisen. There are many directions you can take here: Your affinity for certain meats, cheeses, and flavors will play a major role in how you decide to create your board. Here is one of my favorite boards to make at home.

SERVES 8–10 PEOPLE

INGREDIENTS

FOR THE MEAT

- 6 OZ (170 G) MILD CHORIZO—SLICED INTO ROUNDS (PAGE 52)
- 6 OZ (170 G) SALAMI WITH BEER—SLICED ON BIAS (PAGE 102)
- 6 OZ (170 G) CAMPO SECO—SLICED INTO ROUNDS (PAGE 67)
- 6 OZ (170 G) SALAMI PICANTE—SLICED LENGTHWISE (PAGE 76)
- 6 OZ (170 G) PROSCIUTTO—HAND-SLICED OR SLICED THINLY ON SLICER (PAGE 116)
- MASON JAR OR RAMEKIN OF CHORIZO-INFUSED LARD (BELOW)

SPECIAL TOOLS

- A LARGE SERVING PLATTER (THIS CAN BE A PLATTER, A BOARD, A SLATE, ETC.)
- BASKET FOR BREAD

FOR THE CHEESE

- 5 OZ (142 G) BRIE OR CAMEMBERT-STYLE CHEESE (I RECOMMEND MOSES SLEEPER COW'S MILK CHEESE FROM JASPER HILL FARM IN VERMONT) LEFT WHOLE, WITH SERVING UTENSIL
- 5 OZ (142 G) SEMI-FIRM SHEEP'S MILK CHEESE (I RECOMMEND DANTE FROM THE WISCONSIN SHEEP DAIRY COOPERATIVE), SLICED INTO TRIANGLES
- 6 OZ (170 G) BLUE CHEESE (I RECOMMEND U.S.-MADE ROGUE RIVER BLUE COW'S MILK CHEESE FROM ROGUE CREAMERY), LEFT WHOLE, WITH A SERVING UTENSIL
- 5 OZ (142 G) FIRM GOAT'S MILK CHEESE (I RECOMMEND MADELINE FROM SPROUT CREEK FARM IN NEW YORK), BROKEN INTO BITE-SIZED CHUNKS

ON THE SIDE

- 2 FIG "SALAMIS" (CUT OFF ONE TIP OF THE SALAMI TO ALLOW GUESTS TO SERVE THEMSELVES EASILY) (PAGE 167)
- 2 CUPS (473 ML) FRESHLY TOASTED WALNUTS

BREAD

- 1 WHOLE-WHEAT BAGUETTE—WARMED WHOLE, THEN SLICED ON THE BIAS
- 1 CLASSIC BAGUETTE—WARMED WHOLE, THEN SLICED IN ROUNDS
- PLANTAIN CHIPS

INSTRUCTIONS

1. DIVIDE THE PLATTER INTO 3 SECTIONS, FOLLOWING THE RULES OF THE GOLDEN RATIO (I.E., THE TWO SMALLER THIRDS, COMBINED, ARE EQUAL TO THE LARGEST THIRD).

2. ARRANGE THE MEATS WITHIN THE LARGEST THIRD OF THE PLATTER.

3. ARRANGE THE CHEESE WITHIN ONE OF THE SMALLER SECTIONS OF THE PLATTER.

4. PUT THE FIG "SALAMIS," WALNUTS, AND LARD IN THE SMALLEST THIRD, WITH SERVING UTENSILS.

5. SERVE BREAD AND PLANTAIN CHIPS IN SEPARATE BASKETS BESIDE THE BOARD.

TO MAKE CHORIZO-INFUSED LARD, MELT LARD IN A SAUCEPAN UNTIL JUST LIQUEFIED. STIR DRY-CURED CHORIZO INTO SAUCEPAN SO IT RELEASES ITS OILS INTO THE LARD. THE CHORIZO DOES NOT NEED TO SIMMER, IT JUST NEEDS TO HEAT UP TO ALLOW THE OIL FROM THE CHORIZO TO EFFECTIVELY INFUSE THE LARD. ONCE THE CHORIZO IS WARM, POUR THE LARD AND CHORIZO INTO THE MASON JAR. COVER AND LET STEEP OVERNIGHT. ADD HERBS/SPICES, SUCH AS FRESH THYME, SAGE, ROSEMARY, ROASTED GARLIC, OR STAR ANISE, IF DESIRED.

MEAT:
A BUYER'S GUIDE

Labeling and Claims: A Short List of Basic Considerations for Buying Pork, Beef, and Chicken

Here are some of the things to consider when buying meat. It is important to understand USDA labeling regulations, so you can make more informed meat purchases.

Pork

- Try to choose meat from animals that have been given access to the outdoors.

- Try to choose meat from animals that have not been raised using growth hormones or growth promoters.

- Try to choose meat from animals that have not been administered antibiotics.

- Try to choose meat from animals that have not been given feed containing animal by-products.

- Pork is a red meat, not a white meat, as some marketing campaigns have touted. The redder the meat, the better.

- As of the writing of this book, USDA regulations permit the administration of antibiotics to pigs. However, unlike cows and poultry, pigs must have a "withdrawal" period so that, theoretically, no antibiotic residue is present in the pig at the time of slaughter.

- Although USDA regulations mandate a withdrawal period from antibiotics for pigs, antibiotic-based growth promoters can be administered to pigs without a withdrawal period.

- Be careful when the label says something like this: "Federal regulations prohibit the use of hormones in pork or poultry." It is indeed a good thing that federal regulations prohibit the administration of hormones in pork. That said, make sure to understand that, while the use of hormones is prohibited, there are a host of other "growth promoters" that are indeed permitted.

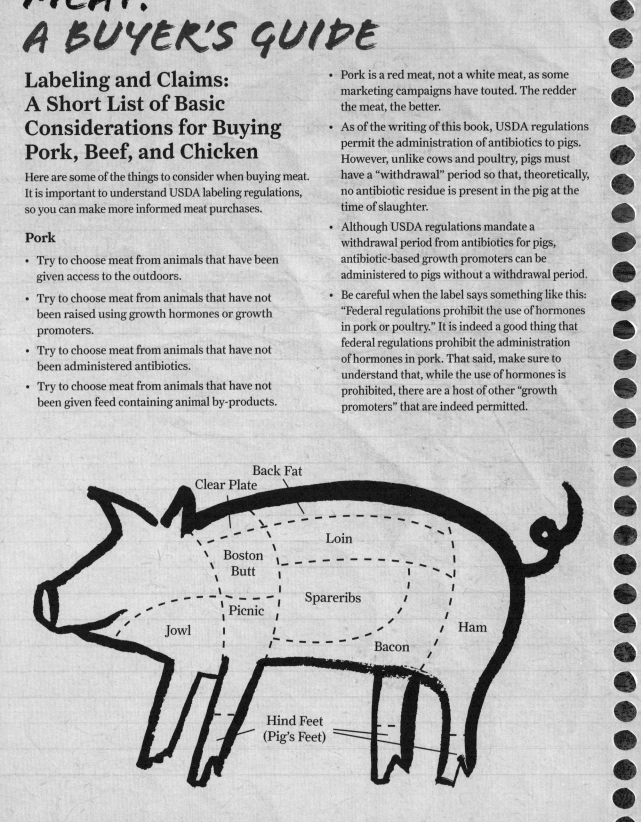

Back Fat

Clear Plate

Loin

Boston Butt

Spareribs

Picnic

Jowl

Ham

Bacon

Hind Feet (Pig's Feet)

Beef

- Try to choose meat that has been grass-fed and grass-finished.

- Beef can be labeled as "grass-fed," even if the cow was fed grains at the end of its life.

- Try to choose meat from animals that have been given access to the outdoors.

- Try to choose meat from animals that have not been administered antibiotics.

- As of the writing of this book, USDA regulations permit the use of hormones in beef cattle. The USDA also permits the use of nonhormone, synthetic growth promoters.

- As of the writing of this book, USDA regulations permit the regular administration of antibiotics until the end of a cow's life in beef cows. This means that when you eat beef from cows that received antibiotics (and, unless the label specifies otherwise, most cows in America do), your meat contains antibiotics as well, which means that when you eat this meat, you are also consuming antibiotics.

Chicken

- Try to choose meat from animals that have been raised with room to move (not in cages).

- Try to choose meat from animals that have been fed an all-vegetarian diet.

- Try to choose meat from animals that have been raised with access to the outdoors.

- Be careful when the label says something like this: "Federal regulations prohibit the use of hormones in pork or poultry." Perhaps the use of hormones is prohibited, but there are a host of other "growth promoters" that can be used, and those don't make their way onto the label.

- As of the writing of this book, USDA regulations permit the regular administration of antibiotics in poultry until the end of the chicken's life. This means that when you eat poultry that received antibiotics (and, unless the label specifies otherwise, most chickens in America do), your poultry contains antibiotics as well. This means that when you eat this poultry, you are also consuming antibiotics.

Cuts and Butchering

One great way to save money on meat and try all cuts is to purchase (either on your own or with a friend) a whole animal. You can break it down and salt it right away or freeze it for later use. It's also a great way to develop a relationship with a farmer of your choice. Your options for where to buy meat will undoubtedly increase if you're open to buying a whole animal, and purchasing half an animal is a great option for smaller appetites and budgets.

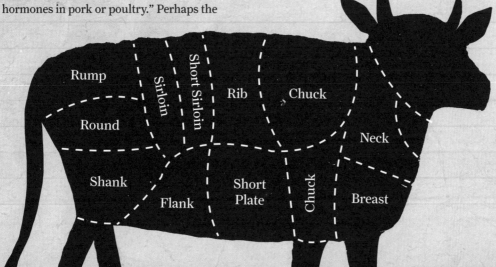

FRESH
SAUSAGE

PURIST SAUSAGE
CLASSIC SALT-AND-PORK SAUSAGE

Yield: 15–20 individual sausages

SPECIAL TOOLS

Sausage stuffer
  (or wide-mouth funnel)
Twine (optional)
Sausage pricker

INGREDIENTS

1.3"–1.4" (34–36 mm)
  hog casings for fresh sausage
1/4 cup (59 ml) white vinegar
7 1/2 lbs (3.4 kg) lean pork
2 1/2 lbs (1.1 kg) fat back (or pork
  belly if you can't find fat back)
2.4 oz (68 g) sea salt

This is a foundation recipe. It's only made of two ingredients—pork and salt—and its minimalist nature is part of its appeal. If you work with quality pork and great salt, this dish is phenomenal on its own. That said, variety is the spice of life, and you can add seasonings to take your sausage in different directions. Treat this as your base and let your imagination run wild.

1. Rinse the casings with cold water, letting water run through them to remove any salt that might be on the inside of the casing.

2. Soak the casings in 8 cups of fresh cold water to 1/4 cup (59 ml) of white vinegar while you prepare the meat mixture. The casings should soak for at least 30 minutes.

3. Chop the meat and fat. Try to keep the meat as cold as possible. If you don't have a grinder for this, you can do it the old-fashioned way, by hand. With a very sharp knife, working quickly, (to keep the meat from warming up and the fat from smearing), chop the meat into 1/4" (6 mm) chunks. The colder the meat/fat is, the easier this will be.

4. Using your hands, mix in the salt. When working with this manageable amount of meat, mixing with your hands is the way to go. If you are quick and swift in the mixing, your hands will generate less heat than an electric mixer, thus helping to keep the meat as cool as possible. You want to evenly distribute the fat and mix in the salt, without overmixing. As soon as you are confident that the ingredients are evenly distributed, stop mixing.

5. Either with a funnel or a sausage stuffer, stuff the meat into the casings, taking care to stuff them tightly, but not so tightly that the casings will break when you twist or tie them into links.

6. Once you have stuffed the casings, you can create the links by **(a)** twisting off the links to your desired size, twisting one link toward you, and the next one away from you, so the links don't become unraveled, or **(b)** taking a little piece of twine and tying off the links by making a knot at your desired link size.

7. Gently prick each link 3 or 4 times with a sausage pricker to remove air bubbles and prevent the casings from bursting while cooking.

8. Fresh sausages are best left to rest for 24 hours in the cooler.

PURIST SAUSAGE, page 45

LONGANIZA CUBANA
CUBAN-STYLE SAUSAGE

Yield: 15–20 individual sausages

SPECIAL TOOLS

Zester or grater

Sausage stuffer
  (or wide-mouth funnel)

Twine (optional)

Sausage pricker

INGREDIENTS

1.3"–1.4" (34–36 mm)
  hog casings for fresh sausage

¼ cup (59 ml) vinegar

7½ lbs (3.4 kg) lean pork

2½ lbs (1.1 kg) fat back
  (can substitute pork belly
  if you can't find fat back)

2.4 oz (68 g) sea salt

1 cup (237 ml) sour orange juice
  (if you don't have sour oranges,
  use equal parts oranges, lemons,
  and limes)

Zest of 1 sour orange

8 garlic cloves, finely chopped

12 oz (340 g) beer (Pilsner style—
  i.e., Presidente)

Longaniza varies widely from region to region, home to home. It is very popular in many parts of Latin America, especially in the Caribbean. It can be found at Latino butcher shops and food markets in a variety of forms. This version is a Cuban style of this famous sausage. My favorite way to eat these is simply—with some bread, grilled on a barbecue in the park, or by the beach with a beer.

1. Rinse the casings with cold water, letting water run through them, to remove any salt that might be on the inside of the casing.

2. Soak the casings in 8 cups of fresh, cold water with ¼ cup (59 ml) of white vinegar while you prepare the meat mixture. The casings should soak for at least 30 minutes.

3. Chop the meat and fat. Try to keep the meat as cold as possible. If you don't have a grinder for this, you can do it the old-fashioned way, by hand. With a very sharp knife, and working quickly to keep the meat from warming up and the fat from smearing, chop the meat into ¼" (6 mm) pieces. The colder the meat/fat is, the easier this will be.

4. Either with your hands or with the paddle attachment of an electric mixer, mix in the salt, sour orange juice and zest, garlic, and beer. The idea here is to mix just enough, without overmixing. As soon as you are confident that the fat is evenly distributed and the ingredients are mixed in, stop.

5. Either with a funnel or a sausage stuffer, stuff the meat into the casings, taking care to stuff them tightly, but not so tightly that the casings will break when you twist or tie them into links. This comes with practice!

6. Once you have the casings stuffed, tie them off into links the length of 2 fingers (around 6" [15 cm]). You can create the links by (a) twisting them off, twisting one link toward you, and the next one away from you, so the links don't become unraveled, or (b) taking a little piece of twine and tying off the links by making a little knot between each one.

7. Gently prick each link 3 or 4 times with a sausage pricker to remove air bubbles and prevent the casings from bursting while cooking.

8. It's best if you let the sausages rest in the refrigerator at least overnight, ideally for 24 hours.

BABY EGGPLANT
THINLY SLICED AND PICKLED, WITH MINCED SAUSAGE
COOKED

Yield: 4 appetizer portions

SPECIAL TOOLS

Mortar and pestle

Mandolin

INGREDIENTS

3 garlic cloves

1 shallot

1 small hot chili pepper

1 teaspoon (5 ml) salt

¼ cup (59 ml) lemon juice

¼ cup (59 ml) rice vinegar

2 lbs (1 kg) baby eggplant
  (green Thai eggplants, if possible)

1 onion, chopped

½ lb (227 g) fresh Longaniza
  Cubana, removed from casing
  (see recipe page 47)

1 cup (237 ml) fresh string beans,
  ends removed, cut into ½"
  (13 mm) pieces

½ cup (118 ml) fresh basil, chopped

¼ cup (59 ml) mint

Pair with an aromatic medium-bodied white such as Riesling or with sparkling wine such as Cava, Cremant, or Prosecco

This dish, if made right, is awesome. It's great on a hot summer afternoon with a cold beer, a warm breeze, and a leisurely mood. Inspired by a Thai eggplant dish, I've come to love the idea of pickling eggplant, a vegetable not typically pickled in the United States. This is not a traditional recipe for Northern Thai Eggplant Salad; rather, it is a variation inspired by that wonderful dish. The trick here is to use baby eggplant, ideally the baby green ones if you can find them, also known as Thai eggplant. If you can't find those, baby purple and baby black eggplants work well.

FOR THE PICKLING LIQUID:

1. Using a mortar and pestle, pound together the garlic, shallot, chili pepper, and salt.

2. Combine lemon juice and rice vinegar, and add this mixture to the garlic, shallot, chili pepper, and salt mixture, to make the pickling liquid.

3. Using a mandolin, thinly slice the eggplants and combine with pickling liquid in a covered container. Shake well to make sure the liquid is evenly distributed over the eggplant. Let pickle for 45 minutes to an hour.

IN THE MEANTIME, PREPARE THE PORK:

1. Sauté the onion over low heat.

2. Add the sausage and sauté until cooked. Just before the sausage is cooked through, turn down the flame and add 2 tablespoons (30 ml) of the pickling liquid to the pan. Mix well and turn off the heat.

PUTTING THE DISH TOGETHER:

1. Remove the eggplant from the liquid and gently squeeze the eggplant dry.

2. Combine the eggplant, the string beans, half of the basil, the solids from the pickling liquid, and a little bit of the pickling liquid to taste. Garnish with the rest of the basil and mint.

BABY EGGPLANT

LAP CHEONG
ASIAN-STYLE SAUSAGE

Yield: 15–20 individual sausages

SPECIAL TOOLS

Sausage stuffer
  (or wide-mouth funnel)
Twine (optional)
Sausage pricker

INGREDIENTS

1.3"–1.4" (34–36 mm) hog casings
  for fresh sausage
¼ cup white vinegar
7½ lbs (3.4 kg) lean pork
2½ lbs (1.1 kg) fat back (you can
  substitute pork belly if you can't
  find fat back)
1³/₄ oz (50 g) sea salt
3 oz (85 g) five-spice powder (equal
  parts star anise, ginger, Sichuan
  pepper, cinnamon, and cloves)
12 oz (340 g) beer
2 oz (57 g) tamari (can substitute
  soy sauce)

Arguably the most internationally known sausage from Asia, Lap Cheung can be found fresh, dried, or smoked in Asian food markets and in Asian dishes across the United States and beyond. This version is a slight variation on the traditional recipe.

1. Rinse the casings with cold water, letting water run through them to remove any salt that might be on the inside of the casing.

2. Soak the casings in 8 cups of fresh cold water with ¼ cup (59 ml) of white vinegar while you prepare the meat mixture. The casings should soak for at least half an hour.

3. Chop the meat and fat. Try to keep the meat as cold as possible. If you don't have a grinder for this, you can do it the old-fashioned way, by hand. With a very sharp knife, and working quickly to keep the meat from warming up and the fat from smearing, chop the meat into ¼" (6 mm) pieces. The colder the meat/fat is, the easier this will be.

4. Either with your hands or with the paddle attachment of an electric mixer, mix in the salt, five-spice, beer, and tamari. The idea here is to mix just enough, without overmixing. As soon as you are confident that the fat is evenly distributed and the ingredients are mixed in, stop.

5. Either with a funnel or a sausage stuffer, stuff the meat into the casings, taking care to stuff them tightly, but not so tightly that the casings will break when you twist or tie them into links.

6. Once you have the casings stuffed, tie them off into 4"–6" (10–15 cm) links. You can create the links by **(a)** twisting them off, twisting one link toward you, and the next one away from you, so the links don't become unraveled, or **(b)** taking a little piece of twine and tying off the links by making a little knot between links.

7. It's best if you let sausages rest in the refrigerator at least overnight, ideally for 24 hours.

MILD CHORIZO
SPICY SPANISH SAUSAGE

Yield: 15–20 individual sausages

SPECIAL TOOLS

Sausage stuffer

Twine (optional)

INGREDIENTS

1.3"–1.4" (34–36 mm) hog casings
   for fresh sausage

¼ cup white vinegar

5 lbs (2.3 kg) lean pork

2½ lbs (1.1 kg) lean beef
   (I like eye round)

2½ lbs (1.1 kg) fat back (you can
   substitute pork belly if you can't
   find fat back)

5 cloves garlic (1 clove garlic per
   2 lbs [1 kg] meat)

3 oz (85 g) sea salt

4.8 oz (136 g) paprika (deep-red
   Spanish paprika Pimenton de la
   Vera is my favorite)

This is the very first sausage I ever made. Thus, the recipe for mild chorizo holds a special place in my heart. The recipe depends on three main ingredients: pork, salt, and paprika. If any one ingredient is lacking in quality, the chorizo will suffer. When I was growing up, my father used to take me to a local Spanish restaurant, where we'd order the "broiled chorizo." It came sliced, slightly brown, with sliced onions broiled alongside the chorizo so they were nice and soft, almost caramelized. Without that chorizo, I probably would not have been inspired to make chorizo at home, and without the experience of making chorizo at home, I probably would not have been inspired to open the business that has, in many ways, forged my identity as an adult. I've tried my best in this recipe to honor the memorably high standard in chorizo that I was lucky enough to experience as a young person with my father.

1. Rinse the casings with cold water, letting water run through them to remove any salt that might be on the inside of the casing.

2. Soak the casings in 8 cups of fresh, cold water with ¼ cup (59 ml) of white vinegar while you prepare the meat mixture. The casings should soak for at least half an hour.

3. Chop the meat and fat. Try to keep the meat as cold as possible. If you don't have a grinder for this, you can do it the old-fashioned way, by hand. With a very sharp knife, and working quickly to keep the meat from warming up and the fat from smearing, chop the meat into ¼" (6 mm) pieces.

4. Finely chop the garlic.

5. Either with your hands or with the paddle attachment of an electric mixer, mix in the salt, paprika, and garlic. I prefer to use my hands, because it heats the meat less than a mixer and I feel more in control of the mixing. The idea here is to mix just enough, without overmixing. As soon as you are confident that the fat is evenly distributed and the ingredients are mixed in, stop.

6. Either with a funnel or a sausage stuffer, stuff the meat into the casings, taking care to stuff them tightly, but not so tightly that the casings will break when you twist or tie them into links.

7. Once you have the casings stuffed, tie them off into the desired links. I like dramatic, long links for the chorizo, about 8" (20 cm) each. If you want to go one traditional Spanish route, you can make them into a U-shape, which would require you to tie (not twist) the links at each end, so that a piece of twine connects both ends, and maintains the U-shape. Otherwise, you can create the links by (a) twisting them off, twisting one link toward you, and the next one away from you, so the links don't become unraveled, or (b) taking a little piece of twine and tying off the links by making a little knot between links. Prick the sausages.

8. It's best if you let the sausages rest in the refrigerator at least overnight, ideally for 24 hours.

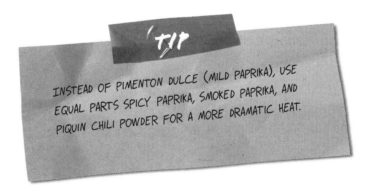

TIP

INSTEAD OF PIMENTON DULCE (MILD PAPRIKA), USE EQUAL PARTS SPICY PAPRIKA, SMOKED PAPRIKA, AND PIQUIN CHILI POWDER FOR A MORE DRAMATIC HEAT.

PAN CON CHORIZO
PRESSED CUBAN SANDWICH WITH CHORIZO
COOKED

Yield: 4 sandwiches

SPECIAL TOOLS
Electric mixer (optional)
Baking sheet (approximately
  13" x 18" [33 x 45.5 cm])
Flat-surfaced sandwich press
  (plancha) or flat-top grill with
  a grill press
Plancha

INGREDIENTS
For the Cuban Bread
2 teaspoons (10 ml) sugar
1¼ cups (296 ml) warm water
1 packet active, dry yeast
2 cups (473 ml) bread flour (you
  can substitute all-purpose flour)
2 cups (473 ml) all-purpose flour
3 teaspoons (15 ml) salt
¼ cup (59 ml) lard

For the Filling
4 fresh chorizos
½ onion, sliced
Fried shoestring potato sticks

For the Chimichurri Sauce
1 cup (237 ml) parsley
1 cup (237 ml) cilantro
2 cloves garlic
Juice from 1 lemon
¼ cup (59 ml) olive oil

There's nothing like a good pressed Cuban sandwich. Although the ubiquitous "Cuban" has been made countless times with countless variations, my criteria will always be good Cuban bread with meat in the middle, grilled on a flat-surfaced plancha. Pan con Chorizo is typically a simple sandwich, but a little extra attention can elevate it to perfection. This recipe calls for homemade bread, which I love and which is not very difficult to make. If you're in a hurry, buy a large loaf of Cuban bread (or French bread in a pinch).

FOR THE CUBAN BREAD:

1. Preheat the oven to 450°F (232°C), with a pan of water in the oven. The pan of water will help create humidity in the oven, which is very beneficial for bread baking.

2. "Wake up" the yeast by mixing the sugar, ¼ cup (59 ml) of lukewarm water, and the dry yeast. Let sit for 15 minutes, or until a frothiness develops on the top (like what you'd see in a glass of beer).

3. While the yeast wakes up, sift the flour and salt together in a mixing bowl. Set aside.

4. Heat the lard in a saucepan, just until melted. Remove from heat, and add 1 cup (237 ml) of lukewarm water to the lard.

5. Add the lard mixture to the yeast mixture and combine.

6. Slowly add the dry ingredients (flour and salt) to the wet ingredients (water, yeast, lard), making sure to stir continuously. Reserve a little bit of flour for rolling out the dough.

7. Knead until the dough is elastic and smooth, about 15 minutes by hand, or 4–5 minutes in an electric mixer outfitted with a dough hook.

8. Once smooth, place the dough into a lightly greased bowl covered with a towel. Let rise in a dark, room-temperature space (about 70°F [21°C]) for 1 hour.

9. When the dough has risen, roll out the dough to ¾" (2 cm) on a lightly floured surface. Rolled-out dough should be about 12" (30.5 cm) wide by 18" (45.5 cm) long.

10. Roll the dough into a tight cylinder. Gently taper off the ends by pinching them and folding them under to form a loaf.

11. Lay the loaf, seam-side down, on the diagonal of the baking sheet (this will ensure the longest loaf possible). Score the top with a razor blade or a sharp knife, first vertically down the middle of the loaf, then horizontally across the middle of the loaf. You should end up with a scored cross.

12. Loosely cover and leave to rise again in a dark place at around 70°F (21°C) (room temperature) for another hour, until your loaf is 2–3 times its original size.

13. Bake for about 15 minutes, or until golden brown.

FOR SANDWICH FILLING

1. Slice chorizos lengthwise, butterflying the sausages (that is, do not cut all the way through). Open the chorizos flat.

2. Lightly sauté the onions. Once they become tender, add the chorizos and cook through.

FOR THE CHIMICHURRI

1. Blend the parsley, cilantro, garlic, lemon juice, and olive oil together in a blender.

TO ASSEMBLE THE SANDWICH

1. Cut the bread into 4 pieces and slice open for sandwiches.

2. Slather chimichurri on both sides of the bread.

3. Lay the butterflied chorizo down the middle of the bread, layering the onions over the chorizos.

4. Preheat the plancha and press the sandwiches on the flat top until golden brown and crispy on both sides.

5. Right before serving, open the sandwiches and spread a handful of potato sticks over the filling. This is a classic take on a Cuban-style sandwich that will add flavor and great texture. A textural detail like this can mean the difference between a very good sandwich, and a standout, memorable one.

WINE PAIRING

Pair with a light- to medium-bodied red, such as a Beaujolais or a young Rioja.

PAN CON CHORIZO, page 54

GRILLED SAUSAGE SKEWERS, page 58

GRILLED SAUSAGE SKEWERS
WRAPPED IN COLLARD GREENS WITH MINT LEAVES
COOKED

Yield: 20 skewers

SPECIAL TOOLS

Wood or bamboo skewers

Charcoal grill

INGREDIENTS

2 fresh chorizos (or fresh sausage
of your choice), meat removed
from the casings

30 mint leaves

Approximately 10 collard green
leaves, cut in half, with center rib
removed

WINE PAIRING

Pair with a medium-bodied red,
such as Barbera or Syrah.

Here's a great dish to serve as an appetizer or finger food. These
skewers can be time-consuming to make, but the end result is totally
worth it. Since this dish requires meat to be cooked inside a leaf, the
leaf acts as a flavor insulator, and really locks in the juiciness of the
meat, the freshness of the mint, and the smokiness of the grill.

1. Shape sausage meat into 1-square-inch (2.5 cm²) patties, ½" (13 mm) thick.

2. Lay 1 meat patty on top of 1 mint leaf, placing both at the bottom edge of
1 half-collard leaf (this will sandwich the mint leaf between the collard
leaf and the meat). Tightly roll the collard green, making sure none of its
contents are exposed. Secure by running a skewer through the middle.

3. Heat up a charcoal grill and grill on each side until the meat is cooked.
Serve hot off the grill.

MORCILLA
BLOOD SAUSAGE

Yield: 15–20 individual sausages

SPECIAL TOOLS
Funnel

Stock pot

Twine (optional)

INGREDIENTS
1.3"–1.4" (34–36 mm) hog casings for fresh sausage

¼ cup white vinegar

1 pound (454 g) pork belly (you can substitute back fat or leaf fat)

1 onion, finely chopped

3 cloves garlic, finely chopped

3 sprigs rosemary, leaves removed, stems discarded, leaves finely chopped

2 oz (57 g) sea salt

5 pounds (2.3 kg) of unsalted pork blood

While I can understand why many people are often squeamish about eating blood sausage, I've never really been able to relate to that. Rich in iron, protein, and flavor, blood sausage is supremely delicious, highly nutritious, and far too valuable a part of the animal to write off. This recipe is a "base morcilla" that you can modify as you wish by adding ingredients for flavor and texture.

1. Rinse the casings with cold water, letting water run through them to remove any salt that might be on the inside of the casings.

2. Soak the casings in fresh, cold water with ¼ cup (59 ml) of white vinegar. The casings should soak for at least 15 minutes.

3. While the casings soak, chop or grind the pork belly into at least ¼" (6 mm) cubes.

4. Cook the onions and garlic over low heat, letting them brown slightly. Once they are tender, add the rosemary and salt. Set aside and let cool.

5. Combine all of the ingredients in a bowl, making sure they are very well-mixed.

6. Tie each of the casings off at one end with twine. Using a funnel that's wide enough for the solid pieces in the mixture to pass through, put the untied end of the casing over the tube of the funnel.

7. With a ladle, spoon the mixture into the funnel until your desired link length is reached, leaving enough room for you to comfortably tie the untied end into approximately 6" (15 cm) links (it is helpful to have two people for this whole process; that way one can hold the funnel while the other ties the links). Carefully tie the open end to prevent the mixture from spilling out of the casing.

8. Place the sausages in boiling water. Cover the stockpot and turn the heat as low as you can. Tightly cover the pot and poach for 15–20 minutes. Check 1 sausage after 15 minutes. You can check by piercing 1 link. If you see any liquid blood, it's not quite done. You can also test if it's done by checking the firmness of the sausage. If it's a bit squishy, it's not yet done. It should feel like the flesh between your thumb and your pointer finger, when your hand is taut. That said, the piercing method is a little more foolproof.

9. You can eat them right away, but my favorite way of eating blood sausage is to allow them cool. Once cool, slice them into ½" (13 mm) thick slices and pan-sear the slices until well-browned. Serve with a little mustard.

THREE WAYS TO COOK A FRESH SAUSAGE WITHOUT DRYING IT OUT

The key to perfectly cooked sausage is never to overcook it. Overcooking causes the fat to render out too much, leaving your sausage dry and crumbly. As the saying goes with salt, "You can always add more, but you can't take it away." You can always cook your sausage more, but once it's overcooked, there's no turning back. Here are three of my favorite ways to cook a sausage.

NOTE: These cooking times are assuming a standard diameter of a sausage link (about 1–1½" [2.5–4 cm]).

Poached, with a Twist

1. BRING A POT OF WATER TO A BOIL.

2. PUT SAUSAGE INTO BOILING WATER.

3. COVER TIGHTLY, AND TURN THE WATER OFF.

4. REMOVE FROM HEAT AFTER 20 MINUTES.

TIP

WHEN POACHING SAUSAGE, IF YOU DON'T FEEL COMFORTABLE TURNING THE HEAT OFF COMPLETELY, YOU CAN LOWER IT TO A SIMMER IN STEP 3, AND CHECK IF THE SAUSAGE IS FINISHED AFTER 15 MINUTES.

Whole, Pan-Seared Sausage in a Cast-Iron Skillet

NOTE: This method works best when cooking a few sausages at a time, filling up the skillet as much as you can without overcrowding.

1. TURN THE HEAT ON AND GET YOUR SKILLET HOT, NOT SMOKING, BUT HOT ENOUGH SO THAT A DROPLET OF WATER SIZZLES ON IT. A FRYING PAN WILL ALSO WORK FOR THIS METHOD.

2. ADD THE SAUSAGES AND LET THEM COOK FOR 30 SECONDS TO 1 MINUTE WITH THE HEAT ON HIGH, LETTING A SEAR FORM.

3. LOWER THE HEAT TO LOW-MEDIUM AND CONTINUE TO SEAR FOR 5 MINUTES ON EACH SIDE, ALLOWING THE SAUSAGES TO BROWN. AFTER BOTH SIDES HAVE COOKED FOR 5 MINUTES, SLICE 1 SAUSAGE OPEN TO MAKE SURE IT'S COOKED THROUGH.

4. LET THE SAUSAGES REST FOR A MINUTE OR 2, THEN EAT.

   BONUS: WITH WHAT'S LEFT ON THE BOTTOM OF THE PAN (I.E., FAT, JUICES, SUCS), YOU CAN SAUTÉ SOME ONIONS—IDEALLY LOW AND SLOW—TO LET THEM CARAMELIZE, TO SERVE ALONG WITH YOUR SAUSAGES. IF YOU DO THIS, YOU CAN KEEP THE SAUSAGES WARM IN A 200°F (93°C) OVEN WHILE YOU SAUTÉ YOUR ONIONS.

Sliced and Seared

1. HEAT A CAST-IRON SKILLET OR FRYING PAN UNTIL HOT (I.E., WHEN A DROP OF WATER SIZZLES ON THE PAN).

2. SLICE SAUSAGES INTO 1/2" (13 MM) SLICES. USE A VERY SHARP KNIFE TO KEEP THE SAUSAGES FROM BREAKING APART WHILE YOU'RE CUTTING THEM.

3. LAY THE SLICES IN THE PAN, AND LOWER THE FLAME TO MEDIUM.

4. SEAR FOR 1 MINUTE ON EACH SIDE.

LARD

My favorite fat to cook with is pork fat, or lard. It is an invaluable cooking ingredient and preservation agent. Lard is simple to make, and you can enhance its flavor by infusing it with herbs and spices. Hard back fat lard is made with the hard fat found underneath the veil of the pig. Soft leaf lard is made from intestinal fat found around the intestines of the pig. Rendered belly fat is the fat found in bacon (that is, bacon grease). I keep a jar of it handy, as it keeps for a very long time, and it is a great cooking fat. Back and belly fat lards are typically used for stovetop cooking (i.e., sautéing, frying, and flavoring liquids), while leaf lard is generally used for baking. If you haven't baked with leaf lard, try it. I clearly remember the first time I had a biscuit made with leaf lard instead of butter. It was one of the most memorable culinary experiences of my life.

Basic Lard ———————————————————— YIELD: 8–9 lbs

This basic lard recipe creates a great staple cooking fat. When the lard is strained, you can return the leftover solids back to the pot or to a skillet so the cracklins can continue rendering and get nice and crunchy. Once crispy, sprinkle them with a little salt and eat as is, or top scrambled eggs, mashed potatoes, or a salad with cracklins (see recipe page 195, for Chicory Salad).

INGREDIENTS

- PORK FAT (AS MUCH AS YOU HAVE—I LIKE MAKING AT LEAST 10 LBS [4.5 KG] AT A TIME; THE RECIPE REALLY DOESN'T CHANGE, ASIDE FROM THE RENDERING TIME)
- WATER
- 1½ OZ (35.5 G) SALT

SPECIAL TOOLS

- COLANDER
- HEAVY-BOTTOMED STOCKPOT OR LARGE DUTCH OVEN
- CHEESECLOTH, CLOTH, OR PAPER TOWEL

INSTRUCTIONS

1. CUT FAT INTO SMALL CUBES.

2. COVER WITH WATER. (IF YOU DON'T USE WATER, THE FAT WILL BURN AND THE LARD WILL TURN COLOR, AND LIKELY SMOKE. DONE RIGHT, THE LARD WITH BE A VELVETY WHITE WHEN IT'S FINISHED AND CHILLED.)

3. SALT TO TASTE.

4. BRING WATER TO A BOIL ON HIGH HEAT. ONCE WATER IS BOILING, COVER THE POT AND LOWER THE HEAT. LEAVE IT ALONE! IT WILL TAKE QUITE SOME TIME TO RENDER, AT LEAST 2–3 HOURS.

5. WHEN YOU SEE CRACKLINS STARTING TO FORM ON THE BOTTOM OF THE POT, THAT MEANS THE WATER HAS EVAPORATED OUT AND IT'S TIME TO STRAIN YOUR LARD. LAYER A COLANDER WITH EITHER CHEESECLOTH OR A PAPER TOWEL, AND STRAIN THE LARD.

6. STORE IN A MASON JAR OR A CROCK.

Chorizos Preserved in Lard _____ YIELD: 3-4 chorizos

INGREDIENTS

- 3-4 CHORIZOS (PAGE 84)
- LARD (ABOUT 1 LB)

SPECIAL TOOLS

- MASON JAR

1. MAKE FRESH CHORIZOS IN 3" (7.5 CM) LINKS (SEE RECIPE PAGE 52).

2. POACH THEM, FOLLOWING THE INSTRUCTIONS ON PAGE 60.

3. PLACE CHORIZOS IN A MASON JAR AND COVER WITH LARD.

4. AFTER 2-3 DAYS, YOUR CHORIZOS BE DELICIOUS, PRESERVED, AND READY FOR A NICE SEAR.
   YOUR LARD IS NOW INFUSED WITH CHORIZO, WHICH WILL ENHANCE ITS FLAVOR AND MAKE
   IT EVEN MORE DELICIOUS, ESPECIALLY SPREAD ON BREAD.

Flaky Tart Crust with Leaf Lard ____ YIELD: 1 tart crust 8"-10"

INGREDIENTS

- 1/2 CUP (118 ML) RENDERED LEAF LARD,
  VERY COLD
- 7/8 CUP (207 ML) FLOUR
- 1 TABLESPOON (15 ML) COLD WATER
- A PINCH OF SALT
- A PINCH OF SUGAR

SPECIAL TOOLS

- DOUGH SCRAPER OR FOOD PROCESSOR
- ROLLING PIN

INSTRUCTIONS

1. CUT RENDERED LARD INTO SMALL CUBES. SET ASIDE.

2. FLOUR THE WORKING SURFACE.

3. ADD THE SALT AND SUGAR TO THE FLOUR. CUT THE LARD INTO THE FLOUR USING A DOUGH SCRAPER OR YOUR
   FINGERS. WORK QUICKLY TO MAKE SURE THE LARD STAYS COLD. STOP WHEN THE MIXTURE IS THE CONSISTENCY
   OF WET SAND (THIS CAN ALSO BE DONE IN A FOOD PROCESSOR WITH A FEW TAPS OF THE "PULSE" BUTTON).

4. ADD THE WATER, AND COMBINE THE MIXTURE INTO A BALL, HANDLING IT JUST ENOUGH TO MAKE IT BIND
   TOGETHER, TAKING CARE NOT TO OVERWORK IT.

5. FLATTEN THE BALL INTO A DISK AND WRAP IT IN PLASTIC. LET IT REST FOR AT LEAST 30 MINUTES,
   UP TO ONE DAY IN THE REFRIGERATOR.

6. IF YOU ARE READY TO ADD YOUR FILLING, YOU CAN ROLL OUT YOUR DOUGH IMMEDIATELY. IF FROZEN,
   THE DOUGH WILL LAST INDEFINITELY.

French Fries in Lard —————— YIELD: 1 basket of fries 2–4 servings

INGREDIENTS

- 3 IDAHO POTATOES
- ENOUGH LARD ONCE MELTED TO COVER POTATOES FOR FRYING
- SALT TO TASTE (APPROXIMATELY 1 TEASPOON [5 ML])

SPECIAL TOOLS

- DEEP-BOTTOMED SKILLET

INSTRUCTIONS

1. CUT POTATOES INTO DESIRED FRENCH FRY THICKNESS. IF YOU'RE NOT FRYING THEM IMMEDIATELY, PLACE THE POTATOES IN WATER TO KEEP THEM FROM BROWNING.

2. IN A DEEP-BOTTOMED SKILLET, HEAT LARD TO APPROXIMATELY 300°F (149°C). THIS TEMPERATURE IS NOT QUITE HOT ENOUGH FOR FRYING, BUT IT IS HOT ENOUGH TO COOK THE POTATOES.

3. THOROUGHLY DRY FRENCH FRIES WITH A KITCHEN TOWEL, IF YOU'VE SOAKED THEM.

4. POACH POTATOES IN THE MELTED LARD UNTIL COOKED AND REMOVE WITH A SLOTTED SPOON, TAKING CARE TO RESERVE THE LARD.

5. RAISE THE HEAT OF THE LARD TO 350°F (177°C), HOT ENOUGH TO FRY AND MAKE THE FRENCH FRIES CRISPY. YOU'LL KNOW IT'S READY WHEN A DROPLET OF WATER SIZZLES IN THE LARD. YOU CAN ALSO TEST IT BY FRYING ONE FRENCH FRY TO SEE IF IT CRISPS UP.

6. FRY THE POTATOES UNTIL GOLDEN BROWN AND CRISPY. SALT TO TASTE.

Warm Bread with Compound Lard —— YIELD: 4 servings

INGREDIENTS

- 1 CUP (237 ML) LARD
- CHOPPED ONIONS
- 4 CLOVES GARLIC, CHOPPED
- 1 SPRIG ROSEMARY, LEAVES REMOVED AND CHOPPED FINELY
- 1 SPRIG THYME, LEAVES REMOVED AND CHOPPED FINELY
- 6 SAGE LEAVES, CHOPPED FINELY
- SALT TO TASTE (APPROXIMATELY 1 TEASPOON [5 ML])
- 1 LOAF OF BREAD

INSTRUCTIONS

1. PREHEAT OVEN TO 350°F (177°C).

2. SOFTEN LARD BY TAKING IT OUT OF THE REFRIGERATOR AND LETTING IT REACH ROOM TEMPERATURE (70°F [21°C]).

3. WHILE THE LARD SOFTENS, SAUTÉ THE ONIONS AND GARLIC WITH THE FRESH HERBS OVER MEDIUM-LOW HEAT, ADDING SALT TO TASTE, LETTING THEM SWEAT AND GET JUST LIGHTLY BROWN. LET THE SAUTÉED MIXTURE COOL.

4. FOLD THE SAUTÉED MIXTURE INTO THE SOFTENED LARD WITH A RUBBER SPATULA, AND MIX UNTIL EVERYTHING IS WELL-INCORPORATED. TASTE THE MIXTURE AND ADD MORE SALT IF DESIRED.

5. PUT THE MIXTURE INTO A SHALLOW MASON JAR OR A RAMEKIN. RETURN IT TO THE REFRIGERATOR AND LET IT SET, IDEALLY OVERNIGHT.

6. PUT A CHUNK OF BREAD (IT COULD BE THE WHOLE LOAF OR A SMALLER PORTION—HOWEVER MUCH YOU INTEND TO SERVE) INTO THE PREHEATED OVEN. LET IT WARM FOR ABOUT 10 MINUTES, OR UNTIL IT'S PIPING HOT IN THE MIDDLE AND HAS A NICE CRUST. REMOVE FROM THE OVEN AND SLICE IT INTO THICK PIECES.

7. SERVE THE WARM BREAD IN A BASKET WITH COMPOUND LARD ON THE SIDE.

DRY-CURED SALAMIS

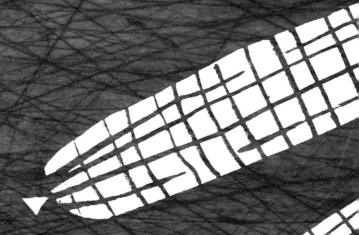

CAMPO SECO
SALT-AND-PORK SALAMI
CURED

10–15 six-oz (170 g) salamis

Sausage stuffer or
  thick-tubed funnel
Twine
Sausage pricker
pH reader

INGREDIENTS

Natural hog casings, packed in
  salt (approximately 44–46 mm in
  diameter or smaller)
7½ lbs (3.4 kg) lean pork shoulder
  or ham, trimmed of any sinew,
  silver skin, or nerves
2½ lbs (1.1 kg) pork back fat
½ packet of starter culture of your
  choice
8 oz (237 ml) spring water (Do not
  use tap water. The chlorine in
  municipal water supplies can kill
  the cultures.)
4.8 oz (136 g) high-quality sea salt
0.8 oz (23 g) pink salt #2 (also goes
  by the name Prague powder #2)

Much like the first fresh sausage recipe (page 45), the recipe that I'm starting off with here is a foundation recipe. It is absolutely delicious on its own and will do the best job of any of these salami recipes of showcasing the integrity and the quality of the pork and the salt that you choose to use.

1. Soak the casings in cold water for at least an hour, changing the water every 15 minutes or so, making sure to clean them completely of salt; 3–4 changes of water should do the trick. Before you're ready to use the casings, run cold water through them once more.

2. Chop or grind the meat and the fat with a super-sharp knife or meat grinder, making sure to keep them very cold to avoid smearing. Chop until the pieces are about ¼" (6 mm) in diameter. If you like a finer texture, grind more finely. Using an inexpensive manual grinder is my preference here.

3. Mix the starter culture with the water. Stir with a spoon and set aside. It should be ready when you've finished the next step.

4. With very clean hands, combine the sea salt, pink salt, and starter culture with the meat and gently massage everything into the mixture. Be careful not to overmix. Keep the meat as cool as possible so it doesn't break down. Adding an ice cube or two to the mixture helps. That said, also make sure the ingredients are well-incorporated. You should be good to go when the pieces of fat just start to lose their shape, and the meat just begins to look stringy, after about 2 minutes or so of mixing.

5. Set the meat mixture aside in a cold place to rest. Cover and let it rest anywhere from 24 to 48 hours.

6. Right before you're ready to stuff, run cold water through the casings, just to be certain you've gotten all the salt out of them.

(continued on page 69)

CAMPO SECO

7. Using a sausage stuffer with a 1" (2.5 cm) tube, make 6"–8" (15–20.5 cm) links (or desired length), and twist off after each link. After twisting, tie off each link, making a loop at the ends to hang.

OR

Find a cylinder with a 1" (2.5 cm) opening on one side. The most cost-effective way of doing this is to get a big bottle with an opening on the bottom (plastic is the easiest for this). *You can also use a wide-tubed funnel.* Put the casings on the spout side and the meat in the cylinder from the bottom. Push the meat into the casing, making sure that the meat is tightly packed into the casing. Make 6"–8" (15–20.5 cm) links (or desired length), and twist off after each link. After twisting, tie off each link, making a loop at the ends, to hang.

8. Using a thin needle or sausage pricker, prick the casings to remove any air bubbles. This step is very important as it **(a)** removes any air bubbles in the salami, which can lead to oxidation and rancidity, and **(b)** allows moisture to escape during the drying process. Moisture trapped inside the salami can lead to spoilage.

9. Before hanging, your salamis should be wet. If they feel dry and it seems as if the casings might break, splash some water on them. The moisture will keep the casings from breaking, and will add humidity to your fermentation room, which is very important.

10. Hang the salamis and ferment at about 75–80°F (24–27°C) and about 80–85 percent relative humidity for approximately 36 to 48 hours, making sure to leave space between the salamis so that they have consistent airflow. If you're using a pH reader, ferment until a pH of 5.3 is reached.

11. Transfer to the drying area and let cure for approximately 1 month, or until desired hardness is achieved. During this process, make sure the curing box/room is dark and the environment is kept consistent, at about 50–55°F (10–13°C), and 60–70 percent relative humidity. Leave the salamis alone.

SKILLET POLENTA
WITH SALAMI AND MELTED CHEESE
COOKED

Yield: One 8" (20 cm) skillet (about 8 servings)

SPECIAL TOOLS
Pot for cooking polenta
Cast-iron skillet

INGREDIENTS
4 cloves garlic, chopped
10 oz (283 g) salami, cubed
¼ cup (59 ml) olive oil, plus more
  for greasing cast-iron skillet
3 cups (710 ml) rich stock (i.e.,
  chicken, pork, duck)
1 cup (237 ml) dry polenta
2 tomatoes, sliced
¼ cup (59 ml) grated parmesan
8 oz (227 g) fresh mozzarella, sliced
  for layering on top

WINE PAIRING

Pair with a macerated white wine
or a medium-bodied red, such as
Syrah or Barbera.

There is a real sexiness to this dish. It's simple, rustic, colorful, and so warming. It's a dish that has to be done in cast iron to really get that crunchy crust on its outside.

1. Preheat the oven to 450°F (232°C).

2. Toast garlic and salami in olive oil, making sure not to burn them.

3. Add stock and bring to a boil. Salt to taste.

4. When stock is boiling, slowly pour in the dry polenta. Be sure to stir during this step to keep the polenta from forming clumps.

5. Stir often, over low heat, until polenta is tender and is the consistency of thick meal.

6. Grease the skillet with olive oil.

7. Pour the cooked polenta into the skillet and layer the tomatoes, sliced fresh mozzarella, and grated parmesan over the top.

8. Lower oven to 375°F (190°C) and bake until cheese is melted and brown, and a crust forms around the sides of the polenta.

MINIATURE DOUGHNUTS
LEAF-LARDED SWEET 'N SALTY SALAMI DOUGHNUTS

COOKED

Yield: 8–10 mini-doughnuts, depending on how much scrap dough you have left

SPECIAL TOOLS

Biscuit cutter

Pastry cutter

Skillet for frying

Sausage pricker

pH reader

INGREDIENTS

Oil (or lard) for frying

½ cup (118 ml) sugar

A healthy pinch of nutmeg

A healthy pinch of cinnamon

Scraps from biscuit dough
  (see page 193 or 194)

2 oz (57 g) salami,
  cut up into tiny bits

WINE PAIRING

Pair with an unoaked crisp white, such as Chardonnay or Chenin Blanc.

Here's what I like to do with the scraps of my biscuit dough. Whether you freeze the scraps of dough for later use, decide to go for a "biscuit and doughnut" spread, or simply want to start with a fresh biscuit dough for these delicious treats, I'm certain you will enjoy them.

1. Heat the oil (or lard) to 350°F (177°C) in the skillet.

2. Mix sugar, nutmeg, and cinnamon, and set aside.

3. With a pastry cutter, work the scraps from the dough into a solid mass, along with the salami, taking care not to overwork the mixture.

4. With your hands, form the dough into a rectangle. Use a little extra flour to dust your work surface if the dough gets too sticky to work with. Cut out small circles from the dough (about ¾" [2 cm]) with a biscuit cutter.

5. In a skillet, fry your "doughnuts" on both sides until golden brown.

6. Toss "doughnuts" in sugar mixture and serve warm.

PICADILLO
STEWED FERMENTED PORK OVER GARLIC RICE
COOKED

Yield: 5 servings

INGREDIENTS
½ recipe for Campo Seco
  (see page 67)
1 onion, halved and thinly sliced
5 cloves garlic, chopped
Olive oil, for frying
2 mild red peppers, in ¼"
  (6 mm) slices
2 cups (473 ml) pitted green olives
1 cup (237 ml) whole tomatoes,
  canned
½ cup (118 ml) fresh cilantro
1 cup (237 ml) white wine
Salt to taste

WINE PAIRING

Pair with a full-bodied red, such as
Zinfandel or Cabernet Sauvignon.

Picadillo is a classic Cuban comfort food, made with either stewed ground beef or a mixture of fresh ground pork and beef. The meat is mixed with spices and served over white rice. This is not a traditional recipe, but a spin-off of it, using fermented ground pork, instead of fresh ground beef. The fermented pork lends a tanginess to the dish, which complements the other flavor components very well. Serve this over white rice. Even though Cuba is a hot, tropical island, I love eating this dish on a cold, New York winter night. It is filling and comforting, with plenty of calories to keep me warm during winter.

1. Prepare the Campo Seco sausage (see page 67), but do not go past the fermentation stage. A 1–2-day fermentation in the oven should do the trick.

2. Empty the meat from the casings into a bowl and set aside.

3. Sauté the onions and garlic in a little bit of olive oil. After 3–5 minutes, add the red peppers, olives, and tomatoes.

4. Add the meat, stirring often to break it apart and avoid clumping, until cooked.

5. Add the wine and let the mixture cook on medium-low heat for 10 minutes.

6. Add cilantro and salt to taste. Serve over Hot, Garlicky Rice (see page 74).

HOT GARLICKY RICE
COOKED

Yield: 4 cups (946 ml)

INGREDIENTS
6 cloves garlic, chopped
¼ cup (59 ml) olive oil
2 cups (473 ml) medium-grain rice
2½ cups (591 ml) water
1 tablespoon (15 ml) salt

This addictive comfort food is a perfect side dish. When you nail the recipe (and it's not as simple as it seems), it's incomparable! It can even take on a new life when incorporated into a Crispy Rice Pie (see next page).

1. Sauté garlic in the oil.

2. Mix in the rice and lightly sauté for a minute or 2.

3. Add the water and salt. Stir thoroughly, and bring to a boil, maintaining the boil until three-quarters of the water has evaporated.

4. Cover and lower the flame. Allow to simmer for 45 minutes on low heat. Leave it alone and don't touch the cover!

5. Remove from heat. Fluff and serve.

CRISPY RICE PIE
WITH SALTED MEAT
AND POACHED EGG

COOKED

Yield: One 8" (20 cm) rice pie

SPECIAL TOOLS
Cast-iron or nonstick skillet
Fish spatula

INGREDIENTS
2 cups (473 ml) leftover, cooked rice

6 oz (170 g) salted meat of your choice (great with salami) (cut into ½" [13 mm] cubes)

4 oz (113 g) fresh mozzarella or your favorite melting cheese

2 eggs

A handful fresh herbs, chopped

Salt to taste (about 1 teaspoon [5 ml])

Olive oil for skillet

Here's a dish my mother made for us often while we were growing up. If there was leftover rice in our refrigerator, be it from home or from takeout, my sister and I could count on its revival the following day into the crunchy, satisfying goodness that is the rice pie.

1. Combine all ingredients, leaving out just one egg.

2. Heat skillet until wisps of smoke rise from the pan.

3. Pour mixture into pan, making a tightly packed, well-formed circle that takes up the entire pan, making sure to keep the rice from sticking to the bottom.

4. Flip when the underside of the pancake is golden brown, and allow to cook on the other side until it is also golden brown.

5. Poach the other egg in simmering water. A splash of vinegar will help to keep the egg from breaking.

6. Serve the rice pie hot, with the poached egg on top.

TIP

THE BEST WAY TO PREVENT RICE FROM STICKING TO YOUR PAN IS TO MAKE SURE THAT YOUR PAN IS EXTREMELY HOT. WHEN I'M MAKING A RICE PIE, I WAIT UNTIL I FEEL THAT A CRUST HAS FORMED ON THE BOTTOM. THEN I TAKE A FISH SPATULA AND RUN IT UNDER THE RICE PIE WITH ONE QUICK MOTION, LOOSENING THE NEWLY FORMED CRUST FROM THE BOTTOM OF THE PAN. I GIVE THE PAN A LIGHT JIGGLE TO ENSURE THAT I'VE SUCCESSFULLY UNSTUCK THE CRUST. ONCE YOU'RE CONFIDENT THAT YOUR PIE IS LOOSE, LOWER THE HEAT, AND BREATHE EASY! YOU CAN BE SURE THAT THE PIE WON'T STICK, AND YOU CAN LET IT CONTINUE TO COOK UNTIL THE CRUST IS BROWN AND CRUNCHY.

SALAMI PICANTE
SPICY SALAMI
CURED

Yield: 1–15 six-oz (170 g) salamis

SPECIAL TOOLS
Sausage stuffer or thick-tubed
 funnel
Twine
Sausage pricker
pH Reader

INGREDIENTS
1.7"–1.8" (44–46 mm), or smaller,
 natural hog casings, packed in salt
7½ lbs (3.4 kg) lean pork shoulder
 or ham, trimmed of any sinew,
 silver skin, or nerves
2½ lbs (1.1 kg) pork back fat
2 oz (57 g) piquin chili—whole or
 powdered
½ envelope of 1 starter culture of your
 choice (I like Chrs. Hansen, F-LC®,
 available at butcher-packer.com)
5 oz (142 g) spring water (Do not
 use tap water. The chlorine in
 municipal water supplies can kill
 the starter culture.)
4.8 oz (136 g) high-quality sea salt
1 cup (237 ml) Cognac
2 oz (57 g) smoked, spicy pimenton
 (paprika)
1 oz (28 g) powdered cayenne pepper
0.8 oz (23 g) pink salt #2
 (aka Prague powder #2)

One of the many things I learned in developing this recipe is how well liquor, with a tinge of sweetness, can work with spicy flavors. We must have gone through 15 or 20 trial batches, with different chilis and spice blends. The "aha" moment came when we added a few shots of cognac to the mixture. The real challenge came in adding spices that have character, not just heat, and that allow the chief characteristics of the salami, pork, and salt to shine through. This recipe meets that challenge, striking a balance between simplicity and originality.

1. Soak the casings in cold water for at least an hour, changing the water every 15 minutes or so. The idea here is the get all the salt off them; 3-4 changes of water should do the trick.

2. Chop or grind the meat, fat, and piquin chilis (if you're using whole chilis) with a very sharp knife or meat grinder, making sure to keep the mixture very cold to avoid smearing, until the pieces are about ¼" (6 mm) in diameter. If you like a finer texture, chop more finely. Using an inexpensive, manual grinder is my preference here.

3. Mix the starter culture with the water. Stir with a spoon and set aside.

4. With very clean hands, combine the sea salt, Cognac, paprika, piquin (if you're using powdered), cayenne pepper, pink salt, and starter culture with the meat and gently massage the mixture. Be careful not to overmix, and to keep the meat as cool as possible, so it doesn't break down. Adding an ice cube or two to the mixture helps. You should be good to go when all ingredients are well-incorporated, and when the pieces of fat just start to lose their shape and the meat begins to look stringy, after about 2 minutes of mixing.

5. Set the meat mixture aside in a cold place to rest. Cover and let it rest anywhere from 24 to 48 hours.

6. Right before you're ready to stuff, run cold water through the casings, just to be certain you've removed all the salt. Using a sausage press with a 1" (2.5 cm) tube (avoid using a grinder/stuffer combination, a Kitchenaid stuffer attachment, or anything with a drive mechanism, because they will smear the meat), make 6"–8" (15–20 cm) links (or desired length), and twist off after each link. After twisting, tie off each link, making a loop at the ends, to hang.

OR
- -
Find a cylinder with a 1" (2.5 cm) opening on one side. The most cost-effective way of doing this is to get a big bottle with an opening on the bottom (plastic is the easiest for this). You can also use a wide-tubed funnel. Put the casings on the spout side and the meat in the cylinder from the bottom. Push the meat into the casing, making sure the meat is tightly packed in the casing. Make 6"–8" (15–20 cm) links (or desired length), and twist off after each link. After twisting, tie off each link, make a loop at the ends, in order to hang.
- -

7. Using a sausage pricker, prick the casings to remove any air bubbles. This step is very important as it removes any air bubbles in the salami (which can lead to oxidation and rancidity) and it allows moisture to escape during the drying process. Moisture trapped inside the salami can lead to spoilage and ruin your salami.

8. Before hanging, your salamis should be wet. If they feel dry or they feel as if the casings might break, splash some water on them. The moisture will keep the casings from breaking and will add humidity to your fermentation room, which is very important.

9. Hang the salamis and ferment at 75–80°F (24–27°C) and 80–85 percent relative humidity for 36 to 48 hours, making sure to leave space between the salamis so that they have consistent airflow. If you're using a pH reader, ferment until a pH of 5.3 is reached.

10. Transfer to the drying area and let the salamis cure for approximately 1 month, or until desired hardness is achieved. During this process, make sure the curing chamber/room is dark and the environment is kept consistent, between 50°F (10°C) and 55°F (13°C), and between 60 percent and 70 percent relative humidity. Leave the salamis alone.

FRESH FETTUCCINE
WITH SALAMI, KALE, AND EGG YOLK
COOKED

Yield: 2 servings

SPECIAL TOOLS

Rolling pin or pasta machine, although the recipe details the hand method, using a rolling pin

Sharp knife or cleaver

INGREDIENTS

For the Pasta

7 oz (200 g) unbleached all-purpose flour

Pinch of salt

1 egg

1 tablespoon (15 ml) cold water

For the Rest

2 cloves garlic, coarsely chopped

Drizzle of good olive oil

8 oz (227 g) country-style salami, cut in half widthwise and sliced thinly

1 sprig rosemary, removed from stem and chopped

8 leaves of kale, chopped

Salt to taste (approximately 1 teaspoon [5 ml])

2 egg yolks

Pinch of coarse salt

Shaved parmesan (optional)

WINE PAIRING

Pair with a medium- to full-bodied red, such as Chianti.

Comparing fresh pasta with dried pasta is like comparing a song on a record with a live performance. Both have the potential to be transformative and memorable, and both have distinctive benefits. Buying dried pasta is quick and easy. That said, making fresh pasta is deceptively simple and is wildly rewarding. This recipe is one example of a lively and enticing dish created with a few basic ingredients and household staples.

PREPARE THE PASTA DOUGH

1. Sift the flour and salt into a bowl.
2. Create a well in the center and put the egg and water in the well.
3. Using your finger to break the yolk, incorporate the flour into the egg. Knead for 10–15 minutes, or until the dough has a smooth surface when rolled into a ball.
4. Cover and let rest in the refrigerator for half an hour.

PREPARE THE DISH

1. Lightly toast the garlic in olive oil in a pan large enough to fit the noodles once cooked.
2. Add the salami and rosemary and sauté on low heat for 5 minutes.
3. Add the kale and cook until tender.
4. Remove from the heat, leave the mixture in the pan, salt to taste, and set aside.

PREPARE THE EGGS FOR THE YOLKS

1. Bring a pot of water to a boil.
2. Place eggs in boiling water. Boil for 6 minutes, then remove the eggs and run them under cold water to stop the cooking process. Set aside.

PREPARE THE PASTA

1. Cut the ball of dough into 2 pieces.

2. On a lightly floured work surface, roll each ball of dough to 2 mm thickness, or until the dough is the desired thickness of your pasta. Keeping the work surface and the rolling pin lightly floured during this process is very helpful.

3. Your rolled-out dough will be in the shape of 2 rough circles. Cut off the edges of each dough circle, creating 2 rectangles, with 1 side being at least 10" (25.5 cm) long for each. Make sure the dough is not sticky or sticking together if folded.

4. Grabbing the short side and rolling down the length of the long side, roll the dough into an even longer rectangle.

5. Using a sharp knife (I use a cleaver for this) and working quickly, cut ¼" (6 mm) strips down the short side of the rectangle.

6. Unravel the pieces quickly, making sure your noodles don't stick together. Use more flour for this, if needed. If possible, proceed to the next step and cook immediately. If not possible to cook immediately, hang the noodles on a rack so they don't stick together.

COOKING AND PREPARING THE DISH

1. Bring a pot of salted water to a boil (should taste like seawater).

2. Put the toppings back on the stove so that they are hot by the time the pasta is cooked.

3. Place the pasta in the salted water, stirring gently at first to keep the noodles from sticking together.

4. Boil for 2–3 minutes.

5. Remove pasta from the water and drain, reserving ½ cup (118 ml) of the pasta water.

6. Place the noodles into the pan with the toppings, along with a couple of spoonfuls of pasta water, and quickly (but gently) incorporate the ingredients, taking care not to overcook the pasta.

7. Plate by dividing the pasta onto 2 dishes.

8. Carefully shell the eggs and remove the whites, without breaking the yolks.

9. Finish each plate with a yolk, a drizzle of good olive oil, and a dash of coarse salt or shaved parmesan.

FRESH FETTUCCINE, page 78

SALAMI "CHIPS"

COOKED

Yield: 2 servings

SPECIAL TOOLS
Skillet or pan for deep-frying

INGREDIENTS
6 oz (170 g) salami, sliced very
   thinly, on a slicer if possible
Oil for frying
½ cup (118 ml) fig mostarda for
   dipping (see recipe page 188)

WINE PAIRING

Pair with light-bodied red, such as
Beaujolais.

This dish was discovered at one of the pop-up food markets we frequent in New York City. One cold weekday evening, when business was slow, our neighbors across the aisle, La Sonrisa Empanadas, motioned to us for a few thin slices of salami. In accordance with our unwritten understanding that we keep each other fed during the long market hours, we obliged. A few minutes later, we received a surprise treat. Ariel, the empanada master, had taken our slices and dropped then in the fryer. The result was salami chips—a delicious snack, appetizer, and a powerful creator of texture in a wide range of main dishes.

1. Fry slices of salami in hot oil in a skillet or pan for deep-frying until they are crispy, but not burned.

2. Remove the salami slices from oil with a slotted spoon and dab them dry with a paper towel to remove excess oil.

3. Serve in a sharing bowl, with mostarda on the side.

YEASTLESS FOCACCIA
FILLED WITH SALAMI, FRESH MOZZARELLA, AND BASIL
COOKED

Yield: Two 8" (20 cm) focaccias

SPECIAL TOOLS
Rolling pin
2 well-oiled 8" (20 cm) cast-iron
  skillets
Basting brush

INGREDIENTS

For Focaccia
2 cups (473 ml) unbleached
  all-purpose flour
Pinch of salt
¾ cup (177 ml) water
¼ cup (59 ml) olive oil
Sea salt to taste

For the Filling
6 oz (170 g) salami, sliced thinly
6 oz (170 g) fresh mozzarella,
  sliced thinly
10 basil leaves

WINE PAIRING

Pair with an unoaked crisp white, such as Chardonnay or Chenin Blanc.

This dish is a beautiful combination of a classic Italian focaccia, a traditional southern savory skillet cornbread, and a flaky, buttery, Indian paratha bread. If you happen to have a wood-fired oven, use it for this recipe.

1. Preheat the oven to 450°F (232°C).

2. Combine flour and salt. Create a well in the middle and add the water and olive oil.

3. Knead for about 10 minutes, until dough is soft and elastic (this can be done by hand or in a food processor or an electric mixer).

4. Cover and let the dough rest for 1 hour.

5. After the dough has rested, divide it into 4 equal-sized balls. Roll out each ball into a disk large enough to cover the surface of the skillet, with a little extra for the edges. Once flattened, fold each disk in half, brush with olive oil, then fold in half again. It should look like a quarter of a circle at this point. Then roll out again into a circle. Repeat twice for each ball of dough.

6. Lay one disk into the skillet, arranging the salami, then cheese, then basil over the dough.

7. Lay a second layer of dough over the filling, and pinch the edges shut.

8. Brush with olive oil and sprinkle sea salt on the focaccia.

9. Poke 3 or 4 holes in the top to allow air to escape during cooking.

10. Repeat steps 6–9 with the other cast-iron skillet for the second focaccia.

11. Put both cast-iron skillets into the oven and, once the oven door is closed, lower the temperature to 425°F (218°C).

12. Bake until golden brown.

LARGE MILD CHORIZO
SPICY SALAMI
CURED

Yield: 5-10 large chorizos

SPECIAL TOOLS

Sausage stuffer
 (or wide-mouth funnel)
Twine
Sausage pricker
Electric mixer with a paddle
 attachment and a large bowl

INGREDIENTS

4 hog bung ends (this is another
 kind of natural casing—larger and
 thicker, but not edible)
15 lbs (7 kg) lean pork shoulder or
 ham, trimmed of any sinew, silver
 skin, or nerves
5 lbs (2.3 kg) pork back fat
½ envelope of 1 starter culture of your
 choice)
10 oz (283 g) spring water (Do not
 use tap water. The chlorine in
 municipal water supplies can kill
 the starter culture.)
9.6 oz (272 g) high-quality sea salt
1.6 oz (45 g) pink salt #2 (aka
 Prague powder #2)
7 oz (200 g) high-quality sweet
 Spanish paprika (pimenton dulce)
20 cloves garlic, chopped
 (1 per pound [454 g])

Size is really a matter of preference. If I'm going to put the work into making salamis at home, I like to make a variety—not all small, not all large, and not all the same. What does a bigger salami mean? In addition to lasting longer (because there is more of it), it will allow you to vary presentation techniques. It's a little easier to slice on a slicer. Perhaps it's a little more conventional on dishes like pizza and sandwiches. At Charlito's Cocina, we make larger salamis for deli counters, sandwich shops, and chefs who request a larger size, arguing that there is less waste (with fewer end pieces) and they are easier to handle. And, aside from their efficient functionality, they look quite beautiful. They are less time-consuming to make when you are making high volumes. I encourage you to also try the other salami recipes in large format, following the procedure below. It's worth it!

1. Soak the casings overnight in cold water, at least once. The idea here is the get all the salt off them and make sure they are well-hydrated.

2. Chop or grind the meat and the fat with a super-sharp knife or meat grinder, making sure to keep them very cold to avoid smearing, until the pieces are about ¼" (6 mm) in diameter. For a finer texture, grind more finely. Using an inexpensive, manual grinder is my preference here.

3. Mix the starter culture with the water. Stir with a spoon and set aside.

4. With very clean hands, combine the sea salt, paprika, garlic, pink salt, and starter culture with the meat and gently massage everything into the mixture. Be careful not to overmix, and to keep the meat as cool as possible, so it doesn't break down. Adding an ice cube or two to the mixture helps. You should be good to go when the pieces of fat just start to lose their shape, and the meat just begins to look stringy, after about 2 minutes of mixing.

5. Set the meat mixture aside in a cold place to rest. Cover and let it rest anywhere from 24 to 48 hours.

6. Right before you're ready to stuff, run cold water through the casings, just to be certain you've removed all the salt.

7. Using a sausage press with a 1" (2.5 cm) tube (avoid using a grinder/stuffer combination, a KitchenAid stuffer attachment, or anything with a drive mechanism, because that will smear the meat), load the casings inside out into the tube (so the smooth side is on the inside) and stuff into 12"–15" (30.5–38 cm) links, twisting each link. Make sure the meat is stuffed tightly into the casing, taking care not to break the casing. After twisting, tie off each link, making a loop at the end of each link for hanging.

8. Using a sausage pricker, prick the casings to remove any air bubbles. This step is very important because it removes air bubbles in the salami that can lead to oxidation and rancidity, and allows moisture to escape during the drying process. Moisture trapped inside the salami can lead to spoilage and ruin your salami.

9. Before hanging, your salamis should be wet. If they feel dry and it seems as if the casings might break, splash some water on them. The moisture will not only keep the casings from breaking, but it will also add humidity to your fermentation room, which is very important.

10. Hang the salamis and ferment at 75–80°F (24–27°C) and 80–85 percent relative humidity (RH) for approximately 48 hours, making sure to leave space between the salamis so that they have consistent airflow.

11. Transfer to the drying area and let cure for at least 50 days, or until desired hardness is achieved. At Charlito's Cocina, we let these cure for 90 days, taking care to make sure that the drying room is kept humid (about 70 percent relative humidity). During this process, monitor the temperature and relative humidity, keeping them as consistent as possible. Make sure the curing box/room is dark and leave the salamis alone. Light can turn your fat rancid.

TIP

I CANNOT OVERSTATE THE IMPORTANCE OF USING HIGH-QUALITY PAPRIKA IN THIS RECIPE. IF PEOPLE TELL YOU THAT PAPRIKA IS ONLY USEFUL FOR IT'S RED COLOR, THEY ARE WRONG! GOOD PAPRIKA HAS AN UNBELIEVABLE AROMA AND FLAVOR AND WILL MAKE ALL THE DIFFERENCE IN YOUR CHORIZO.

SALAMI "CHIPS," page 82

LARGE MILD CHORIZO, page 84

CROQUETAS DE CHORIZO
FRIED POTATO AND SALAMI DUMPLINGS
COOKED

**Yield: approximately
16 croquettes**

SPECIAL TOOLS

Pot for boiling potatoes

Hand potato masher (or fork)

Skillet for deep-frying

INGREDIENTS

For Croquettes

Salt to taste

4 potatoes

½ cup (118 ml) olive oil

½ cup (118 ml) whole milk

8 oz (227 g) dry-cured chorizo, cut
  into ¼" (6 mm) cubes

For Frying

Oil for frying

2 eggs

2 tablespoons (30 ml) water

½ cup (118 ml) flour

1 cup (237 ml) panko bread crumbs

WINE PAIRING

Pair with a light to medium-bodied
red, such as Beaujolais or young
Rioja.

There are so many different ways to make croquettes. Not only can you fill them with just about anything, but the foundation for this tasty finger food can be made from a variety of ingredients: Béchamel, potatoes, white beans, and cassava, to name just a few. Since I'm a sucker for keeping things simple and old-fashioned, my go-to croquette uses a potato base with minimal ingredients. Although the recipe here calls for chorizo, these can be done with just about any kind of meat—cured, fresh, or left over, not to mention vegetables.

1. Fill pot with cold, salted water (water should taste like seawater). Bring to a boil.

2. Peel potatoes and slice widthwise to prepare for boiling. Submerge potatoes in pot and boil them until tender.

3. When tender, remove potatoes from water and place in a mixing bowl.

4. Use a potato masher (or a fork—I use a fork) to smash the potatoes, mashing in olive oil and milk.

5. Add the cubed chorizo and smash/mix until the ingredients are well-incorporated. Form the mixture into 2" x 1" (5 cm x 2.5 cm) ovals.

6. Heat oil for frying to 350°F (177°C) in a skillet and set aside.

7. Beat the eggs together with 2 tablespoons (30 ml) of water.

8. One at a time, gently coat each croquette in the flour, then the egg mixture (be careful not to drench them), then the bread crumbs.

9. Fry on all sides until golden brown.

PAELLA
ONE-PAN RICE AND CHICKEN DISH
COOKED

Yield: 4 servings

SPECIAL TOOLS
Paella pan (referred to as a "paella")

INGREDIENTS
¼ cup (59 ml) olive oil

Salt to taste (approximately
  2 tablespoons [30 ml])

6 chicken legs (drumsticks and
  thighs separated)

5 cloves garlic

1 onion, halved and sliced thinly

1 cup (237 ml) fresh, shelled fava
  beans (you can substitute dry
  beans, if fresh not available)

1 teaspoon (5 ml) saffron

¼ cup (59 ml) white wine

16 oz (454 g) dry-cured chorizo
  (sliced, on a bias, ¼" [6 mm] thick)

3 tomatoes (peeled and grated on a
  cheese grater, to make a rough purée)

2 cups (473 ml) chicken stock

2 sprigs rosemary

1 tablespoon (15 ml) sweet Spanish
  paprika (pimenton dulce)

1 cup (237 ml) white rice

4 long strips of preserved red
  peppers (for garnish)

Pair with a rosé or a light-bodied
red, such as Pinot Noir.

When I was growing up, I used to go to a restaurant with my father when we wanted to hang out, just the two of us. It was a classic Spanish place, nestled on a side street in Manhattan. They served a paella that occupies a warm place in my memory: While not presented in a traditional paella pan, it was absolutely delicious, and it still conjures up lovely memories of dinners with my father. My mother's paella didn't always use chorizo, but theirs did. Both were delicious, but I wouldn't feel right not including this recipe, with chorizo, in this book.

1. Heat the oil in the paella on high heat.

2. Sprinkle salt on the chicken and sear until nicely browned. Lower the heat to medium to prevent the chicken from burning.

3. Add the garlic, onions, and fava beans to the paella and cook until the onions are tender.

4. Push the contents of the pan off to the side, so that a small portion of the bottom of the pan is exposed. On this portion, add and lightly toast the saffron, then incorporate it into the rest of the ingredients in the paella.

5. Add the wine, deglazing the paella (scraping the bits off the bottom) and letting it cook for 5 minutes on medium-high heat.

6. Add chorizo and tomatoes and cook another 5 minutes.

7. Add the stock, rosemary, and paprika, and cook until stock is reduced by about 25 percent.

8. Remove the rosemary, taste the stock, and add salt to taste.

9. Add rice and stir thoroughly, making sure the rice is evenly distributed throughout the stock.

10. Let simmer until the liquid is evaporated and the rice is tender. If the liquid evaporates before rice has finished cooking add more stock, little by little (water will do if you run out of stock). Do not cover!

11. Serve hot. Garnish with 4 long strips of preserved red peppers.

POTAJE

POTAJE
HEARTY STEW
WITH CHORIZO
COOKED

Yield: 6 servings

SPECIAL TOOLS
Heavy-bottomed skillet or pan
Stockpot

INGREDIENTS
½ cup (118 ml) chickpeas

½ cup (118 ml) white beans

½ cup (118 ml) black beans

Salt to taste (at least 2 tablespoons
 [30 ml])

½ lb (227 g) pork shoulder

1 lb (454 g) beef short ribs, bone on

½ lb (227 g) pork belly, cut into
 1" (2.5 cm) cubes

½ cup (118 ml) rum

1 quart (0.95 l) chicken stock

½ cup (118 ml) puréed tomatoes

1 bottle Pilsner beer

1 onion, sliced

4 cloves garlic, chopped

1 bay leaf

12 oz (340 g) dry-cured chorizo,
 halved lengthwise, and cut into
 ¾" (2 cm) pieces

1 bunch collard greens

1 bell pepper, diced

½ lemon

Pair with a medium-bodied red,
such as Syrah or Primitivo.

"Potaje" is a general term that refers to any hearty, soupy stew with beans, vegetables, and meats. It's a "kitchen sink" soup, an ideal meal in winter, and a great way to make a big pot of something that's got plenty of nourishment and can last for days. Its variations are only as limited as your imagination—this version includes three kinds of beans, dry-cured chorizo, stewed meats, hearty greens, and fresh sausage.

1. Soak the beans overnight in salted water.

2. Sprinkle salt over the pork shoulder, short ribs, and pork belly, and brown in a heavy-bottomed skillet or pan until well-browned.

3. Deglaze the pan with the rum, making sure to scrape off all the bits from the bottom of the pan.

4. Add the stock, tomatoes, and beer, and turn the flame to low.

5. Drain the beans and set aside.

6. Use your stockpot to sauté the onions, bell pepper, garlic, bay leaf, and pork belly. When the onions are tender and browning, add the drained beans and the chorizo and let the mixture cook for 5 minutes on medium heat, giving it 2 or 3 stirs during those 5 minutes.

7. Then add the stock and beer and stir well, incorporating any bits stuck to the bottom of the pan. Make sure all the meats are covered in liquid. Add water, if necessary.

8. Bring to a boil, cover, and lower to a simmer for at least 2 hours. The longer you let it cook, the more flavorful it will be.

9. Taste and add salt, if desired.

10. Five minutes before serving, add the collard greens to the pot. Cook until just tender, making sure greens maintain their bright-green color. Serve with a squeeze of lemon.

SPANISH TORTILLA
OMELET WITH CHORIZO
COOKED

Yield: One 8" (20 cm) tortilla (about 6 slices)

SPECIAL TOOLS
8" (20 cm) skillet or nonstick pan

INGREDIENTS
1 potato

¼ cup (59 ml) + 1 tablespoon (15 ml) olive oil

6 oz (170 g) dry-cured chorizo, cut into ¼" (6 mm) cubes

6 eggs

Salt to taste

2 tablespoons (30 ml) water

½ yellow onion

WINE PAIRING

Pair with a sparkling wine, such as Cava, Crémant, or Prosecco.

Tortilla is highly versatile. Arguably the national dish of Spain, tortilla is an "any time of the day food." It's a satisfying breakfast, an ideal midmorning snack, a sandwich that's filling at lunch, a mid-afternoon pick-me-up, and a comforting, yet not overly filling, way to wind down the day at dinner. Delicious eaten hot or cold, it's hard to go wrong with this classic dish. The consummate comfort food, this is my go-to dish for sharing among friends, starting off a lazy Sunday morning, or even putting together a quick, light dinner with the promise of breakfast leftovers the following morning.

1. Peel potato and cut into quarters, lengthwise, creating four spears. Slice into ½" (13 mm) slices.

2. Heat enough oil to completely cover all the potatoes in an 8" (20 cm) skillet.

3. Poach potatoes, yellow onion, and chorizo in the oil, ensuring that the temperature is hot enough to cook the potatoes, but not so hot that it will fry them (about 300°F [149°C]). Make sure that all the potatoes are covered in oil. The idea is to get them soft. This takes about 10 minutes.

4. While the potatoes and chorizo are poaching, beat the eggs with a pinch of salt, 1 tablespoon (15 ml) olive oil (this will help keep the eggs from sticking to the pan), and 2 tablespoons (30 ml) of water (this will help lighten the texture of the tortilla). Set aside.

5. When the potatoes are finished, remove and reserve half of the oil, leaving the potatoes and chorizo in the pan (the idea is to have a healthy coating of oil in the pan but not so much that the tortilla is swimming in oil).

6. Making sure the pan is very hot, pour the eggs over the contents of the pan, stirring gently, to make sure the potatoes and chorizo are evenly distributed, and that the eggs aren't sticking to the pan. Let the tortilla cook until lightly brown, taking care to make sure the eggs do not stick to the pan.

7. Once they're lightly brown, and making sure the tortilla isn't stuck to the pan, put a plate over the skillet and quickly flip it so the uncooked side is facedown on the plate. This step should be done as quickly and carefully as possible.

8. Add a little more olive oil to the pan to prevent the tortilla from sticking, and gently slide the tortilla, uncooked side down, back into the pan.

9. Cook for another 3–4 minutes, until the other side is lightly brown.

10. Remove onto a serving platter (plate, board, etc.). Let cool and slice carefully into 6 slices.

SLOW SCRAMBLED EGGS
WITH SALAMI AND SAGE
COOKED

Yield: 1 serving

SPECIAL TOOLS
Frying pan

INGREDIENTS
3 eggs

10 sage leaves, chopped

3 oz (85 g) dry-cured salami (chorizo is my favorite) (cut into ½" [13 mm] cubes)

1 tablespoon (15 ml) olive oil

1 tablespoon (15 ml) water

WINE PAIRING

Pair with a sparkling wine, like Champagne or Prosecco, or a medium-bodied red, such as Barbera.

I woke up one Sunday morning with nothing but some eggs and half of a dry chorizo in my refrigerator. When I set off to scramble the two together, I discovered that the flame on my stove would not go higher than its lowest setting. Frustrated, but resigned to the extra 10 or 15 minutes it might take to make breakfast, I hovered over the stove, stirring, waiting for the eggs to cook. The ensuing dish was the creamiest, most satisfying plate of eggs I can remember. Not only were the eggs creamy, porridge-like, and delicious, but the longer cooking time allowed the chorizo to break down a bit and become more tender. This was indeed a happy accident! The key to this dish is low and slow. If you try to rush it, it'll end up as something else.

1. Beat the eggs, sage, salami, olive oil, and water together.

2. Pour the mixture into a pan and place on the stove.

3. Turn heat to medium, stirring continuously with the rubber spatula.

4. At the very first sign that the eggs have started to coagulate, turn the heat to low.

5. Continue stirring gently until the eggs are cooked. You'll notice them slowly continuing to coagulate.

6. Remove from the heat and plate. Serve slightly runny, taking care not to overcook the eggs.

SALAMI WITH HAZELNUTS AND BOURBON

CURED

Yield: Ten 6-oz (170 g) salamis

SPECIAL TOOLS

Meat grinder

Sausage stuffer or thick-tubed funnel

Twine

Sausage pricker

INGREDIENTS

Natural hog casings, packed in salt (approximately 44–46 mm in diameter or smaller)

7½ lbs (3.4 kg) lean pork shoulder or ham, trimmed of any sinew, silver skin, or nerves

2½ lbs (1.1 kg) pork back fat

¼ envelope of 1 starter culture of your choice

8 oz (237 ml) spring water (Do not use tap water. The chlorine in municipal water supplies can kill the starter culture.)

4.8 oz (136 g) high-quality sea salt

0.8 oz (23 g) pink salt #2 (aka Prague Powder #2)

2 cups (473 ml) whole roasted hazelnuts

1 cup (237 ml) bourbon (my favorite for this is Buffalo Trace)

When I first sliced into and took a bite of one of our salamis with hazelnuts, and I saw those beautiful rounds of whole hazelnuts scattered throughout the red, salted goodness, it was a wonderful moment for me. Charlito's Cocina started running this product as a seasonal special back in 2012, and it was a great success. The oaky, fiery, and ever-so-slightly sweet sensation of the bourbon, along with the crunchy, blanched-like texture of the hazelnuts, help to make this salami distinct.

1. Soak the casings in cold water for at least an hour, changing the water every 15 minutes or so. Make sure to rinse off all the salt; 3–4 changes of water should do the trick.

2. Chop or grind the meat and the fat with a super-sharp knife or meat grinder, making sure to keep them very cold to avoid smearing, until the pieces are about ¼" (6 mm) in diameter. For a finer texture, grind more finely. Using an inexpensive, manual grinder is my preference here.

3. Mix the starter culture with the water. Stir with a spoon and set aside.

4. With very clean hands, combine the sea salt, bourbon, hazelnuts, pink salt, and starter culture with the meat and gently massage everything into the mixture. Be careful not to overmix, and to keep the meat as cool as possible, so it doesn't break down. Adding an ice cube or two to the mixture helps. You should be good to go when the pieces of fat just start to lose their shape, and the meat just begins to look stringy, after about 2 minutes of mixing.

5. Set the meat mixture aside in a cold place to rest. Cover and let it rest anywhere from 24 to 48 hours.

6. Right before you're ready to stuff, run cold water through the casings, just to be certain you've gotten all the salt out of there.

7. Using a sausage press with a 1" (2.5 cm) tube (avoid using a grinder/ stuffer combination, or anything with a drive mechanism, because they will smear the meat), make 6"–8" (15–20 cm) links (or desired length), and twist off after each link. After twisting, tie off each link, making a loop at the ends to hang.

OR:

Find a cylinder with a 1" (2.5 cm) opening on one side. The most cost-effective way of doing this is to get a big bottle with an opening on the bottom (plastic is the easiest for this). You can also use a funnel and a wide, flexible plastic tube. Put the casings on the spout side and the meat in the cylinder from the bottom. Push the meat into the casing, making sure the meat is tightly packed in the casing. Make 6"–8" (15–20 cm) links (or desired length), and twist off after each link. After twisting, tie off each link, making a loop at the ends to hang.

8. Using a thin needle or sausage pricker, prick the casings to remove any air bubbles. This step is very important as it removes air bubbles in the salami, which can lead to oxidation and rancidity, and allows moisture to escape during the drying process. Moisture trapped inside the salami can lead to spoilage and ruin your salami.

9. Before hanging, your salamis should be wet. If they feel dry and it seems as if the casings might break, splash some water on them. The moisture will keep the casings from breaking and will add humidity to your fermentation room, which is very important.

10. Hang the salamis and ferment at 75–80°F (24–27°C) and 80–85 percent relative humidity for 36 to 48 hours, making sure to leave space between the salamis so that they have consistent airflow. If you're using a pH reader, ferment until a pH of 5.3 is reached.

11. Transfer to the drying area and let cure for approximately 1 month, or until desired hardness is achieved. During this process, make sure the curing chamber/room is dark and the environment is kept consistent, between 50°F (10°C) and 55°F (13°C), and between 60 percent and 70 percent relative humidity. Leave the salamis alone.

EASTERN-STYLE SALAMI

CURED

Yield: Ten 6-oz (170 g) salamis

SPECIAL TOOLS

Meat grinder

Sausage stuffer
 or thick-tubed funnel

Twine

Sausage pricker

INGREDIENTS

Natural hog casings, packed in
 salt (approximately 44–46 mm in
 diameter or smaller)

7½ lbs (3.4 kg) lean pork shoulder
 or ham, trimmed of any sinew,
 silver skin, or nerves

2½ lbs (1.1 kg) pork back fat

¼ envelope of 1 starter culture of
 your choice

8 oz (227 g) spring water (Do not
 use tap water. The chlorine in
 municipal water supplies can kill
 the starter culture.)

3¾ oz (106 g) high-quality sea salt

5 oz (142 g) five-spice (equal parts
 star anise, ginger, Sichuan pepper,
 cinnamon, and cloves [page 37])

2 oz (57 g) tamari (you can
 substitute soy sauce)

1 cup (237 ml) baijiu (Chinese
 distilled spirit made from sorghum)

0.8 oz (23 g) pink salt #2 (aka
 Prague powder #2)

When I was a kid, my parents used to take us to New York City's Chinatown every Sunday. We'd order a whole variety of Chinese foods, from boneless duck's feet to sea cucumber to jellyfish. We ate the most delicious roast duck I've ever tasted and much more. This transformative ritual was beyond fun for me: It was the first time I can remember taking an active interest in food. This salami is a nod to those days.

There are various versions of the liquor in this particular recipe. Although Chinese distilled spirits are difficult to find in many parts of the United States, if you can find real baijiu, a distilled spirit made from sorghum, it's very much worth using.

1. Soak the casings in cold water for at least an hour, changing the water every 15 minutes or so. Make sure to rinse off all salt; 3–4 changes of water should do the trick.

2. Chop or grind the meat and the fat with a super-sharp knife or meat grinder, making sure to keep them very cold to avoid smearing, until the pieces are about ¼" (6 mm) in diameter. For a finer texture, grind more finely. Using an inexpensive, manual grinder is my preference here.

3. Mix the starter culture with the water. Stir with a spoon and set aside.

4. With very clean hands, combine the sea salt, five-spice, tamari, baijiu, pink salt, and starter culture with the meat and gently massage everything into the mixture. Be careful not to overmix, and to keep the meat as cool as possible, so it doesn't break down. Adding an ice cube or two to the mixture helps. You should be good to go when the pieces of fat just start to lose their shape, and the meat just begins to look stringy, after about 2 minutes of mixing.

5. Set the meat mixture aside in a cold place to rest. Cover and let it rest anywhere from 24 to 48 hours.

6. Right before you're ready to stuff, run cold water through the casings, just to be certain you've removed all the salt.

7. Using a sausage press with a 1" (2.5 cm) tube (avoid using a grinder/ stuffer combination, or anything with a drive mechanism, because they will smear the meat), make 6"–8" (15–20 cm) links (or desired length), and twist off after each link. After twisting, tie off each link, making a loop at the ends, to hang.

OR

Find a cylinder with a 1" (2.5 cm) opening on 1 side. The most cost-effective way of doing this is to get a big bottle with an opening on the bottom (plastic is the easiest for this). You can also use a funnel and a wide, flexible plastic tube. Put the casings on the spout side and the meat in the cylinder from the bottom. Push the meat into the casing, making sure the meat is tightly packed in the casing. Make 6"–8" (15–20 cm) links (or desired length), and twist off after each link. After twisting, tie off each link, making a loop at the ends, to hang.

8. Using a thin needle or a sausage pricker, prick the casings to remove any air bubbles. This step is very important as it removes air bubbles in the salami, which can lead to oxidation and rancidity, and allows moisture to escape during the drying process. Moisture trapped inside the salami can lead to spoilage and ruin your salami.

9. Before hanging, your salamis should be wet. If they feel dry and it seems as if the casings might break, splash some water on them. The moisture will keep the casings from breaking and will add humidity to your fermentation room, which is very important. Hang the salamis and ferment at 75–80°F (24–27°C) and 80–85 percent relative humidity for 36 to 48 hours, making sure to leave space between the salamis so that they have consistent airflow. If you're using a pH reader, ferment until a pH of 5.3 is reached.

STEAMED RICE CAKE

IN BANANA LEAF STUFFED WITH GREEN LENTILS, QUAIL EGGS, YOUNG SALAMI, AND FRESH HERBS

COOKED

Yield: Ten 6-oz (170 g) salamis

INGREDIENTS

1 cup (237 ml) green lentils

2 cups (473 ml) salted water

½ cup (118 ml) capers

¼ cup (59 ml) pitted olives, cut in half

5 sprigs each sage, parsley, and thyme, removed from stems and chopped

Salt to taste (about 1½ teaspoons [7.5 ml])

4 quail eggs

Six 20" (51 cm) squares of banana leaf

1 cup (237 ml) sticky rice

16 oz (454 g) young salami of your choice, peeled and cut into cubes (young salami is more moist than fully dried salami, and has only been dried for about a week)

Pair with a sparkling wine, such as Cava, Crémant, or Prosecco.

This rice cake was inspired by a Vietnamese dish, banh chung, which is synonymous with the Vietnamese New Year. This variation is made with ingredients found more commonly in Western cuisine, including salami. It's great just cut into squares and eaten fresh, but my favorite way to eat it is as a leftover. Let's say you eat about half the dish when it's freshly made, and save the other half for the next day. Cut it into slices when it's cold and pan-sear each slice on a hot cast-iron skillet. Serve alongside something acidic, like pickles, or a nice chutney or mostarda. It is awesome.

1. Soak the lentils in water overnight.

2. Once lentils have soaked, bring to a boil in 2 cups (473 ml) salted water, then lower to simmer until water is evaporated and lentils are soft.

3. Mash cooked lentils into a paste, incorporating the capers, olives, and herbs. Season with salt to taste.

4. Boil the quail eggs for 3 minutes, peel, and set aside.

5. Place 2 overlapping banana leaf squares on a flat surface, one placed squarely in front of you, the second rotated 90°, so it looks like a diamond.

6. Scoop half the rice into a mound in the middle of the leaf. Follow that with half the lentil mash, then the salami, then the other half of the lentils, then the other half of the rice.

7. Fold all 4 sides over the filling, as if wrapping a gift, forming a square shape.

8. Repeat the wrapping twice, with the other 4 leaves, 2 leaves at a time, making sure each layer is laid out as in step 5. It's essential that water not penetrate the leaves during boiling. So 3 wraps should give your center a good enough shield.

9. Truss with twine.

10. Cover in cold water and boil on a low flame for 8 hours.

11. Remove from water, let cool, unwrap, and cut into triangles or squares.

12. Serve with pickled onions, shallots, or carrots.

STEAMED RICE CAKE

CERVEZA SECA
BEER SALAMI
CURED

About ten 6-oz (170 g) salamis

SPECIAL TOOLS
Meat grinder

Sausage stuffer or thick-tubed funnel

Twine

Sausage pricker

INGREDIENTS
Natural hog casings, packed in salt (approximately 44–46 mm in diameter or smaller)

7½ lbs (3.4 kg) lean pork shoulder or ham, trimmed of any sinew, silver skin, or nerves

2½ lbs (1.1 kg) pork back fat

½ envelope of 1 starter culture of your choice

8 oz (237 ml) spring water (Do not use tap water. The chlorine in municipal water supplies can kill the starter culture.)

4.8 oz (136 g) high-quality sea salt

12 oz (340 g) high-quality, brown ale—I recommend a big-bodied, robust, boldly flavored beer for this.

0.8 oz (23 g) pink salt #2 (aka Prague powder #2)

While Europe is known for having some of the best places to drink wine in the world, the United States is quickly emerging as one of the world's leading beer producers. Much of the charcuterie made in Europe showcases the award-winning wines of the region. With a plethora of small batch beer being brewed across America, why not create charcuterie that celebrates the abundance of high-quality beer here? It is this thought process that gave way to what is now one of our best-selling salamis—Cerveza Seca—dry-cured salami with beer. One of the lessons I learned in our beer salami experiments is that bold beer does better in salami than lighter beers. Because salami is dry and beer is wet, expect to lose a significant amount of the actual beer in the drying process. That said, the more flavor and the more intensity a beer has, the more powerfully those elements will come across when the salami is ready.

1. Soak the casings in cold water for at least an hour, changing the water every 15 minutes or so. Make sure to rinse off all salt; 3–4 changes of water should do the trick.

2. Chop or grind the meat and the fat with a super-sharp knife or meat grinder, making sure to keep them very cold to avoid smearing, until the pieces are about ¼" (6 mm) in diameter. For a finer texture, grind more finely. Using an inexpensive, manual grinder is my preference here.

3. Mix the starter culture with the water. Stir with a spoon and set aside.

4. With very clean hands, combine the sea salt, beer, pink salt, and starter culture with the meat and gently massage everything into the mixture. Be careful not to overmix, and to keep the meat as cool as possible, so it doesn't break down. Adding an ice cube or two to the mixture helps. You should be good to go when the pieces of fat just start to lose their shape, and the meat just begins to look stringy, after about 2 minutes of mixing.

5. Set the meat mixture aside in a cold place to rest. Cover and let it rest anywhere from 24 to 48 hours.

6. Right before you're ready to stuff, run cold water through the casings, just to be certain you've removed all the salt.

7. Using a sausage press with a 1" (2.5 cm) tube (avoid using a grinder/stuffer combination, or anything with a drive mechanism, because they will smear the meat), make 6"–8" (15–20 cm) links (or desired length), and twist off after each link. After twisting, tie off each link, making a loop at the ends to hang.

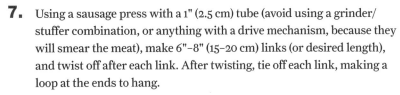

OR

Find a cylinder with a 1" (2.5 cm) opening on one side. The most cost-effective way of doing this is to get a big bottle with an opening on the bottom (plastic is the easiest for this). You can also use a funnel and a wide, flexible plastic tube. Put the casings on the spout side and the meat in the cylinder from the bottom. Push the meat into the casing, making sure the meat is tightly packed in the casing. Make 6"–8" (15–20 cm) links (or desired length), and twist off after each link. After twisting, tie off each link, making a loop at the ends to hang.

- -

8. Using a thin needle or a sausage pricker, prick the casings to remove any air bubbles. This step is very important as it removes air bubbles in the salami, which can lead to oxidation and rancidity, and allows moisture to escape during the drying process. Moisture trapped inside the salami can lead to spoilage and ruin your salami.

9. Before hanging, your salamis should be wet. If they feel dry and it seems as if the casings might break, splash some water on them. The moisture will keep the casings from breaking and will add humidity to your fermentation room, which is very important. Hang the salamis and ferment at 75–80°F (24–27°C) and 80–85 percent relative humidity for 36 to 48 hours, making sure to leave space between the salamis so that they have consistent airflow. If you're using a pH reader, ferment until a pH of 5.3 is reached.

10. Transfer to the drying area and let cure for approximately 1 month, or until desired hardness is achieved. During this process, make sure the curing chamber/room is dark and the environment is kept consistent, between 50°F (10°C) and 55°F (13°C), and between 60 percent and 70 percent relative humidity. Leave the salamis alone.

WILD MUSHROOM SALAMI
WITH GARLIC AND GIN
CURED

Yield: 4 servings

SPECIAL TOOLS

Meat grinder
Sausage stuffer
  or thick-tubed funnel
Twine
Sausage pricker

INGREDIENTS

Natural hog casings, packed in
  salt (approximately 44–46 mm in
  diameter or smaller)
7½ lbs (3.4 kg) lean pork shoulder
  or ham, trimmed of any sinew,
  silver skin, or nerves
2 ½ lbs (1.1 kg) pork back fat
12 oz (340 g) coarsely chopped
  Chanterelle Mushrooms (or your
  favorite wild mushroom/s)
10 cloves garlic, finely chopped
A few leaves of chopped rosemary
4.8 oz (136 g) high-quality sea salt
1 cup (237 ml) of your favorite
  American craft gin
0.8 oz (23 g) pink salt #2 (aka
  Prague powder #2)
¼ envelope of 1 starter culture of
  your choice
8 oz (237 ml) spring water (Do not
  use tap water. The chlorine in
  municipal water supplies can kill
  the starter culture.)

The production of distilled spirits is growing rapidly in the United States. A pungent, floral gin imparts fantastic character into a salami. In addition to enhancing its flavor profile, alcohol is, generally speaking, a good thing for salami. It has antimicrobial properties and will improve the chances that the salami will turn out well while helping to prevent the meat from spoiling. With chanterelles now gaining in popularity in the United States and grown throughout many regions of the country, chances are you'll be able to find them in most specialty food markets. If you can't get your hands on any chanterelles, use your favorite fresh wild mushroom in this recipe. The most important quality of mushrooms is their freshness. If you're lucky enough to know a mushroom hunter in your area who has a sweet spot for chanterelles, offer her or him a trade of salami in exchange for mushrooms.

1. Soak the casings in cold water for at least an hour, changing the water every 15 minutes or so. Make sure to rinse off all salt; 3–4 changes of water should do the trick.

2. Chop or grind the meat and the fat with a super-sharp knife or meat grinder, making sure to keep them very cold to avoid smearing, until the pieces are about ¼" (6 mm) in diameter. For a finer texture, grind more finely. Using an inexpensive, manual grinder is my preference here. Place meat in freezer or refrigerator while doing step 3.

3. Sauté the chanterelles and garlic, along with the rosemary. Let cool and set aside.

4. Mix the starter culture with the water. Stir with a spoon and set aside.

5. With very clean hands, combine the sea salt, sautéed mushroom mixture, gin, pink salt, and starter culture with the meat and gently massage everything into the mixture. Be careful not to overmix, and to keep the meat as cool as possible, so it doesn't break down. Adding an ice cube or 2 to the mixture helps. You should be good to go when the pieces of fat just start to lose their shape, and the meat just begins to look stringy, after about 2 minutes of mixing.

6. Set the meat mixture aside in a cold place to rest. Cover and let it rest anywhere from 24 to 48 hours.

7. Right before you're ready to stuff, run cold water through the casings, just to be certain you've removed all the salt.

8. Using a sausage press with a 1" (2.5 cm) tube (avoid using a grinder/stuffer combination, a KitchenAid stuffer attachment, or anything with a drive mechanism, because they will smear the meat), make 6"–8" (15–20 cm) links (or desired length), and twist off after each link. After twisting, tie off each link, making a loop at the ends, to hang.

OR

Find a cylinder with a 1" (2.5 cm) opening on one side. The most cost-effective way of doing this is to get a big bottle with an opening on the bottom (plastic is the easiest for this). You can also use a funnel and a wide, flexible plastic tube. Put the casings on the spout side and the meat in the cylinder from the bottom. Push the meat into the casing, making sure the meat is tightly packed in the casing. Make 6"–8" (15–20 cm) links (or desired length), and twist off after each link. After twisting, tie off each link, making a loop at the ends, to hang.

9. Using a thin needle or sausage pricker, prick the casings to remove any air bubbles. This step is very important as it removes air bubbles in the salami, which can lead to oxidation and rancidity, and allows moisture to escape during the drying process. Moisture trapped inside the salami can lead to spoilage and ruin your salami.

10. Before hanging, your salamis should be wet. If they feel dry and it seems as if the casings might break, splash some water on them. The moisture will keep the casings from breaking and will add humidity to your fermentation room, which is very important. Hang the salamis and ferment at 75–80°F (24–27°C) and 80–85 percent relative humidity for 36 to 48 hours, making sure to leave space between the salamis so that they have consistent airflow. If you're using a pH reader, ferment until a pH of 5.3 is reached.

11. Transfer to the drying area and let cure for approximately 1 month, or until desired hardness is achieved. During this process, make sure the curing chamber/room is dark and the environment is kept consistent, between 50°F (10°C) and 55°F (13°C), and between 60 percent and 70 percent relative humidity. Leave the salamis alone.

EARTHENWARE-BAKED WHITE BEANS
WITH SALAMI, GREENS, AND CHEESE
COOKED

Yield: 4 servings

SPECIAL TOOLS
Earthenware dish or oven-safe
  baking dish

INGREDIENTS
2 cups (473 ml) white beans,
  dry (you can substitute canned
  beans—just make sure to rinse
  them well)
6 cups (1.4 l) water
8 oz (227 g) salami of your choice,
  cubed
4 oz (113 g) grated pecorino or
  parmesan
8 oz (227 g) fresh mozzarella,
  cut into ½" (13 mm) cubes
1 bunch lacinato kale,
  well-chopped
4 cloves garlic, chopped
1 tablespoon (15 ml) olive oil
About 10 sage leaves, well-chopped
Salt to taste (approximately
  1 teaspoon [5 ml])

WINE PAIRING

Pair with a macerated white wine
or an aromatic white.

This is a delicious, nourishing, and filling dish that's great to have on a cold night with nice, toasty bread and a glass of bourbon. It takes very little time to prepare, and is a "kitchen-sink" dish that is highly satisfying.

1. Soak the white beans in water for at least an hour, preferably overnight. When soaking has finished, boil until tender and drain.

2. Preheat oven to 450°F (232°C).

3. Combine beans, salami, pecorino/parmesan, half the mozzarella, kale, garlic, olive oil, and sage, and toss until all ingredients are well-combined. Salt to taste.

4. Place in an earthenware dish and top with the remaining mozzarella.

5. Bake at 450°F (232°C) until the mozzarella is melted and browning.

WHOLE MUSCLE

DRY-CURED LOMO

PROSCIUTTO

MOJAMA

LARDO

BRESAOLA

BUILDING THE WHOLE-MUSCLE BOARD

In the seemingly endless variety and combinations of charcuterie boards, it seems worthwhile to focus on the least adulterated form of cured meats—the whole muscle. In its purest form, whole-muscle charcuterie is made from an intact piece of meat that has been salted and air-dried. No grinding, no stuffing, just simple salting and hanging. Just as whole-muscle cured meats are made in the spirit of being hands-off, this board can be brought together in that same spirit—hands-off, simple, and letting the stars of the plate do the talking.

SERVES 4-6 SERVINGS ON 1 PLATE

INGREDIENTS

- 2 OZ (57 G) PROSCIUTTO, SLICED THINLY
- 1 OZ (28 G) LARDO, SLICED THINLY
- 2 OZ (57 G) BRESAOLA, SLICED THINLY
- 2 OZ (57 G) LOMO, SLICED THINLY
- 2 OZ (57 G) MOJAMA, SLICED THINLY
- 6 OZ (170 G) FRESH, IN-SEASON FIGS, QUARTERED (YOU CAN SUBSTITUTE SWEET MELON FOR THE FIGS, IF YOU CAN'T FIND FRESH FIGS)
- 1/2 CUP (118 ML) MARCONA ALMONDS
- 1/2 CUP (118 ML) CASTELVETRANO OLIVES
- 1/2 CUP (118 ML) PICKLES (OPTIONAL)
- 1/2 FRESHLY BAKED, PEASANT LOAF (WITH GOOD CRUST AND CHEWY INSIDE) (OPTIONAL)
- HANDFUL OF VERY THIN BREADSTICKS (GRISSINI)

SPECIAL TOOLS

- PLATTER OR BOARD
- MEAT SLICER
- DISH FOR THE OLIVES
- DISH FOR THE PICKLES
- PLATTER FOR BREAD
- CLEAR GLASS JAR OR VASE FOR BREADSTICKS

INSTRUCTIONS

1. RESERVE TWO-THIRDS OF THE PLATTER FOR THE MEAT, ONE-THIRD FOR THE NONMEATS, AND MAKE UP A SEPARATE PLATTER FOR THE BREADS.

2. ARRANGE THE PROSCIUTTO AND LARDO SO THAT THE SLICES AREN'T OVERLAPPING, RUFFLING EACH SLICE TO BOTH SAVE SPACE ON THE PLATTER AND GIVE THE PROSCIUTTO SOME VOLUME, MAKING SURE THAT THEY DON'T TAKE UP MORE THAN TWO-FIFTHS OF THE MEAT SECTION.

3. ARRANGE BRESAOLA, LOMO, AND MOJAMA IN THIN SLICES ON THE REST OF THE MEAT SECTION.

4. PLATE THE QUARTERED FIGS, ALMONDS, OLIVES, AND PICKLES IN THE REMAINING SPACE. PLATE THE OLIVES AND PICKLES IN THEIR OWN DISH.

5. ON A SEPARATE PLATTER OR IN A BREAD BASKET, PLATE THE PEASANT BREAD IN A MOUND, WITH THE GRISSINI IN A CLEAR GLASS JAR NEXT TO IT ON THE SAME PLATE. SERVE THAT NEXT TO THE MAIN BOARD.

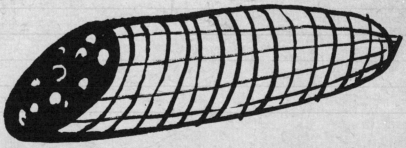

WHOLE MUSCLES: A BUYER'S GUIDE

- Know the producer—understanding who raised your meat is essential. Know what their standards are, what quality of feed they source, and what their general approach as a producer is. The quality of life of any animal will affect the quality of their meat. It's helpful to familiarize yourself with the people behind the brands that you see in your local markets. If there are producers you know and feel comfortable with whose products are not available where you shop, request them.

- Choose meats that have vibrant colors—this is usually a sign of quality.

- If the appearance/aesthetics of your board is important to you, choose a variety of cuts—some wide, some narrow, some marbled, some lean. This will allow you more room for creativity in presentation.

- Keep it simple and enjoy! Don't let whole muscle purchases stress you out.

LOMO EMBUCHADO
CURED PORK TENDERLOIN
CURED

Yield: 2 lomos

SPECIAL TOOLS
Pyrex dish or Tupperware® large
  enough to fit the loin
Netting or twine for trussing
Sausage pricker
A weight for the meat
A clean, damp cloth

INGREDIENTS
Sea salt to cover loin
1 loin of pork, trimmed of its silver
  skin and sinews, leaving a small
  fat cap where there is fat
10 cloves of garlic, finely chopped.
2 tablespoons (30 ml) olive oil
8–12 sprigs rosemary
10–15 sprigs thyme
Sweet Spanish paprika as
  needed—about 2 cups (473 ml)
  (recommended: Pimenton de la
  Vera, dulce)
2 hog bung ends

I love this dish. Lomo is lean and meaty, and it can be used in so many different ways (see, for example, Family-Style Noodles on page 114). Keep in mind that since lomo is one of the leaner meats, it will lose a large percentage of its weight in the drying process. The fattier a meat is, the less weight it loses in the drying process, because fat has almost no water activity. A lomo embuchado can dry quite efficiently, so unlike prosciutto you can enjoy it within a month or so.

1. Put a layer of salt on the bottom of your container. Place the loin on top of the salt.

2. Cover the loin with salt and let it rest for about 12 hours in the refrigerator. The longer you leave it, the saltier it will be. It's better to continue the salting process for a longer period, as you need to be sure that the salt has penetrated to the center of the meat. If it hasn't, your meat runs the risk of spoiling.

3. After a 12-hour rest period, rinse off the salt in cold water, making sure to remove it all. Cut the loin in half lengthwise, so you're left with 2 long pieces. This will also allow you to check if the salt has penetrated to the center. If the center is still soft and fleshy, it needs more time in the salt. The texture of the meat at this point should feel like the flesh between your thumb and pointer finger when your hand is taut.

4. Make a paste with the garlic, olive oil, and paprika (see the tip on the next page). Massage the paste into the loin, making sure to rub it in well and not miss any spots. After massaging the paste into the meat, cover the outside of the loin with the herbs.

5. Place the loin into a clean dish, cover with a clean, damp cloth, and let it rest in the refrigerator for 4 days, turning the loin every day to make sure the paste is evenly distributed.

6. Cover the dish with a clean, damp cloth and let it rest in the refrigerator for 4 days, turning the loin every day to make sure the paste is evenly distributed.

7. On the third day of refrigeration, soak the casings in cold water, changing the water at least twice. Make sure to remove all the salt from the casings. Since these casings are quite thick, they are best soaked overnight.

8. On day 4, remove the loin from the refrigerator. Gently rinse off the paste and discard the herbs. Rinse the casings thoroughly, running water through them. Stuff the loin into the casing. Simply slip each piece into the casing and tie one end off tightly and securely with twine. Then, holding the other end, spin the casing a few times, to make sure the meat is tightly packed in (think cowboy with a lasso). Tie the other end. Prick with a pricker to release any air bubbles that might have formed.

9. Hang in a cool, humid, place for about 25 days, or until the loin is your desired hardness. The ideal temperature for this is around 50°F (10°C).

TIP

THE EASIEST WAY TO MAKE A GARLIC, OLIVE OIL, AND PAPRIKA PASTE IS TO USE A MORTAR AND PESTLE. YOU CAN ALSO DO THIS WITH A CHEF'S KNIFE, BY CHOPPING THE INGREDIENTS TOGETHER, THEN PRESSING THEM INTO YOUR CUTTING SURFACE WITH THE FLAT SIDE OF THE KNIFE. SCRAPE THE INGREDIENTS BACK INTO A TIGHT PILE, AND REPEAT. EACH TIME YOU REPEAT THIS CYCLE, YOUR MIXTURE WILL BECOME MORE PASTE-LIKE.

FAMILY-STYLE NOODLES
BUCATINI WITH THINLY SLICED LOMO, ABUNDANT GREENS, AND CRUNCHY CHICKPEA CRISPS

COOKED

Yield: 4 servings

INGREDIENTS

3 cloves fresh garlic, chopped

4 oz (113 g) oyster mushrooms, coarsely chopped

½ cup (118 ml) fresh arugula

½ cup (118 ml) pea shoots (when in season)

½ cup (118 ml) fresh radicchio

6 fresh basil leaves

2 sprigs fresh thyme, leaves removed from stem

12 oz (340 g) bucatini (or thick noodles of choice)

1 soft poached egg

2–3 tablespoons (30–45 ml) vinegar

Olive oil

Salt to taste

5 thin slices of dry-cured lomo

For Chickpea Crisp

¼ cup (59 ml) chickpea flour

¼ cup (59 ml) water

Pinch of salt

1 teaspoon (5 ml) olive oil

WINE PAIRING

Pair with a medium-bodied aromatic white, such as a dry Riesling.

I love noodles. The reason I don't eat them as often as I crave them is that they are so filling and tend to weigh me down if I overdo it. This dish provides the simple solution: While the noodles are the foundation of the dish, they don't make up the majority of the plate. In this case, abundant greens, crunchy chickpea crisps, and just enough protein give this dish a variety of textures and flavors that satisfy without becoming too heavy.

1. Sauté garlic and mushrooms and set aside.

2. Prepare salad by combining arugula, pea shoots, radicchio, basil, and thyme. Set aside.

3. Boil pasta in well-salted water and cook until al dente. When finished, drain and toss in olive oil, mushrooms, garlic, and salt to taste. Set aside.

4. Combine chickpea flour, water, and salt. Stir until smooth with no lumps. Stir in the olive oil, and allow to rest for 5–10 minutes.

5. While the chickpea dough is resting, poach the egg in simmering water with 2–3 tablespoons (30–45 ml) vinegar (the vinegar will keep the egg from breaking), for 1–2 minutes, making sure not to overcook the egg. The idea is to cook the white, and leave the yolk runny. Set aside and reserve for plating.

6. On a well-oiled, hot skillet, make a chickpea "pancake," as thin as you can without breaking it. Cook until golden brown and flip. Cook the other side until golden brown.

TO PLATE

1. In a large bowl meant for sharing, plate the pasta on one-third, the salad on one-third, and the lomo on one-third, nestling the chickpea crisp vertically between the pasta and the salad.

2. Top the pasta with the poached egg, a sprinkle of salt, and a drizzle of olive oil.

FAMILY-STYLE NOODLES

PROSCIUTTO
CURED LEG OF PORK
CURED

Yield: 2 lomos

SPECIAL TOOLS
Large hotel pan or area to
 rest ham while salting
Rope

INGREDIENTS
1 whole rear leg of pork—skin on,
 bone in, and, ideally, foot still
 attached
Sea salt to cover
Lard
Buckwheat flour (you can
 substitute cornmeal or
 all-purpose flour)

Dry-cured rear leg of pork, also known as prosciutto, jamon, jambon, or ham, is considered one of the pinnacles of the charcuterie world. It takes a long time to make —at least one year—so patience is of the essence. It's also important to recognize that, after a year or more of waiting, your ham might not turn out as expected. For this reason, I recommend attempting this recipe with more than one ham, so when they're done you'll have more than just one sample to work with. When you're trying to figure out the optimum temperatures at which to dry your ham, consider the climates where dried hams are most famous— Parma, Italy, or Salamanca, Spain. Take a look at the weather patterns there. Mountainous, temperate, and humid climates are ideal for making this dish. If you happen to live in a similar climate, fantastic. If not, keep that in mind when drying the ham. These regions rarely experience temperatures below freezing. Take into account the misty mornings of fall and the warmer, sunnier periods during the daytime hours. Many of the best hams are dried in areas that are resistant to changes in temperature (i.e., a cave or a cellar). Make sure your drying place is always dark. Overexposure to light will turn the fat rancid.

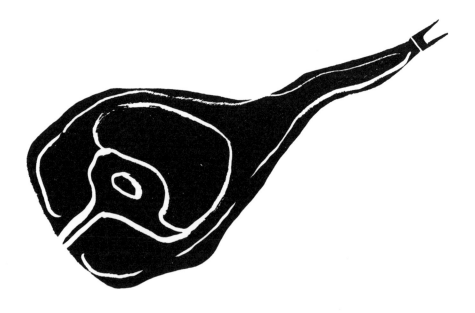

1. **Salt:** Make 1 layer of salt on the bottom of your dish. Place your ham into the dish, skin/fat side down. Cover the ham with salt, taking care to not miss any spots. Get into the cracks, around the bone, and where any air bubbles might be. Remember that the salt will draw out moisture and reduce the weight of the ham, which means that areas around the bone are especially prone to meat pulling away and forming air bubbles, which will make the ham spoil. A thorough and consistent salting is essential to the process. Also keep in mind that the salt must penetrate all of the meat and, since one side of the ham is covered in skin, the salt must be applied only in the areas where meat is exposed. Make sure to apply enough salt to penetrate all the way through the ham, to the skin. Leave the dish to rest in the refrigerator for 1 day per 2 pounds (1 kg) of meat (i.e., an 18 lb [8 kg] ham = 9 days in salt).

2. **Rinse:** With cold water, rinse off any excess salt and soak the ham in cold water, in the refrigerator overnight. Remove from water and pat dry.

3. **Rest:** Let the ham rest for 2–3 days in the refrigerator.

4. **Hang:** Tie a knot around the hoof of the leg with the rope and hang it in a cold, dark place (35–40°F [1.5–4°C]) for 2 months. After 2 months, raise the temperature and keep it at about 50–55°F (24–27°C), maintaining the humidity at about 60–70 percent. Leave it for another 4 months. At this point, it's important to make sure that the part of the ham with the meat exposed isn't too dry. Naturally, the inner parts of the ham will take longer to dry, so this is where the lard and buckwheat flour come in. A paste is rubbed over the exposed parts of the meat, to keep them from getting too dry, before the rest of the ham dries. To do this, make a paste out of equal parts lard and buckwheat flour, enough to cover the parts of the ham that are exposed. Rub the paste over these parts so that they are covered with about a ¼" (6 mm) layer of paste.

5. Let the ham hang for another 6 months, or longer, if desired. The longer you leave it, the more the flavor will develop. I like to leave it at least 18 months, or up to 2 years.

PROSCIUTTO, page 116

PROSCIUTTO, page 116

PROSCIUTTO AND MELON

COOKED

Yield: 12 pieces

SPECIAL TOOLS

Plate for serving
Toothpicks (optional)

INGREDIENTS

13 thin slices of prosciutto
A ripe, in-season melon, cut in
  half, peeled, seeded, and sliced
  into half moons

Simple cooking with great-quality ingredients can yield some of the best food in the world. When a prosciutto is done well, and a melon is at its peak of ripeness, there are very few things that can elicit the satisfaction that this dish does. Try substituting fresh figs for melon as a delicious variation, or drizzling olive oil and freshly ground pepper over the top to add additional dimensions of flavor.

1. Taste a piece of prosciutto, then a piece of melon. It will feel so good.

2. Wrap each piece of melon with a slice of prosciutto.

3. Arrange on a platter and serve as is, with a toothpick in each piece, if you'd like.

BREAKFAST TOAST
WITH CURED MEAT, FIG, AND CHEESE
COOKED

Yield: 2 toasts

SPECIAL TOOLS

A toaster oven or a standard oven

INGREDIENTS

4 slices fig "salami"

2 slices of the best whole-grain
  bread you can find

2 thin slices prosciutto

4 slices brie or camembert cheese
  (I like Moses Sleeper cheese from
  Jasper Hill Farm in Vermont)

This dish came about as a result of a barter we started with a Vermont-based cheesemaker. We send them a box of salami every month in exchange for a box of cheese. Our newfound bounty of cheese inspired us to find new ways to enjoy cheese and meat together. This recipe calls for prosciutto, but you can feel free to use the cured meat of your choice with any cheese that melts well. With dry-cured meats and warm, melty cheese, you really can't go wrong!

1. Smear the fig "salami" on the bread.

2. Layer the prosciutto, then the cheese on top of the fig "salami."

3. Toast until the cheese begins to melt and the bread forms a nice crust.

PROSCIUTTO AND MELON, page 120

BRESAOLA
DRY-CURED EYE ROUND OF BEEF
CURED

Yield: 1 dry-cured eye round

SPECIAL TOOLS

Pyrex dish or Tupperware large
  enough to fit meat
A weight for the meat
Netting or twine for trussing
Sausage pricker

INGREDIENTS

Salt
1 cup (237 ml) juniper berries
Pink salt #2
1 top round or eye round of beef
  (both work well)
7 sprigs rosemary
Beef bung cap casing, 4½"
  (11.5 cm) in diameter

This is my favorite dry-cured beef dish. It's mellow and just beefy enough. If you're able to use beef from a grass-fed and -finished cow, do it. Not only will you taste the beef as it's intended to be, but your bresaola will have an unparalleled richness. Make this to vary the array of items on your charcuterie board, to have something to slice off for a quick sandwich on your way to work in the morning, or for your nonpork-eating friend or relative. When finished, bresaola is most commonly eaten sliced thinly, as thick slices can get a little salty.

1. Mix together the salt, juniper berries, and pink salt to make a rub.

2. Massage the rub very well into the meat, taking care not to miss any spots, getting into every little crack and crevice.

3. Cover the outside of the meat with the rosemary sprigs and wrap very tightly in plastic wrap. A covered Pyrex container will work if you don't like working with plastics.

4. Place a weight over the meat and let it sit in the refrigerator for 15 days, turning it every 2 days to make sure that everything is covered and that the cure is penetrating evenly.

5. After 15 days, prepare your casing by rinsing thoroughly and soaking it in cold water overnight.

6. Rinse the salt cure off the meat in cold water and pat dry. Stuff the meat into the casing and tie one end off tightly and securely with twine. Then, holding the other end, spin the casing a few times, to make sure the meat is tightly packed in (think cowboy with a lasso). Tie the other end.

7. Truss or put the encased meat in netting and prick it a few times on each side with a pricker, to remove any air bubbles. Hang in a cool place (approximately 50°F [10°C]) for about a month.

8. When ready to serve, slice thinly and enjoy!

BRESAOLA

SKILLET FRITTERS
WITH WHITE BEANS, MIXED GREENS, AND BRESAOLA

COOKED

Yield: One 8" (20 cm) skillet cake

SPECIAL TOOLS

Hand masher
8" (20 cm) cast-iron skillet or
  nonstick pan

INGREDIENTS

3 garlic cloves, peeled and thinly
  sliced
Olive oil for sautéing
3 cloves garlic, chopped
1 cup (237 ml) soaked, softened
  white beans
¼–½ cup (59–118 ml) rich stock
  (i.e., chicken, pork, etc.)
Salt to taste
Juice from 1 lemon
1 cup (237 ml) mixed salad greens
  of your choice
1 tablespoon (15 ml) olive oil for
  greens
3–4 oz (85–113 g) thinly sliced
  bresaola (cut into strips)

This isn't a pancake in the conventional sense, but it is a good way to put together a filling and healthy meal with some cured meat. In this case, we use bresaola—air-dried, salted beef. Try miniature versions of these as appetizers.

1. Simmer the beans for at least ½ an hour in the stock.

2. Peel and thinly slice 3 cloves of garlic.

3. Toast them in olive oil until just brown and crunchy. Set aside for plating.

4. Lightly brown the other 3 garlic cloves (chopped) in a pan with a little olive oil.

5. Drain the beans. Combine with 3 cloves chopped garlic, salt, and juice from half a lemon. Mash with a hand masher until it forms a pliable mixture that can be shaped. Taste for seasoning and adjust to your taste.

6. Form into a disk shape and pan-fry on both sides, until golden brown. The pancake should have a nice crust on both sides. If you want a little extra crust, dust each side in flour.

7. While the pancake is cooking, lightly coat the greens with olive oil, juice from the other half of the lemon, and salt to taste.

8. Plate the pancake first, topped with the greens and the bresaola, and finished with the sliced, toasted garlic.

SALT PORK

CURED

Yield: As many pork scraps as you have

SPECIAL TOOLS
Pyrex dish or container
 large enough to fit meat
A weight for the meat

INGREDIENTS
Pork fat and/or fatty
 scraps of pork
Salt

Salt pork is great for cooking. It's not meant to be eaten raw. The idea here is to preserve the raw meat, hence the high salt content. If you find it's too salty when you go to cook with it, soak it in cold water to leech out the salt, then dry it well before cooking with it. You can get an idea of how well pork packed in salt keeps in the classic John Steinbeck novel *The Grapes of Wrath.* Before embarking on an epic and mysterious trip west, the Joad family slaughters their two pigs, lets the meat rest overnight, and trusts that the pork will keep in salt as long as they need it to. As Pa remarks, "Tomorra we'll get that pork salted early in the morning, an' then we'll get the truck loaded, all but the beds, an' nex' morning off we'll go.*

1. Coat pork fat with salt, cover with a piece of parchment paper or plastic wrap, and place it in a large container. Place a weight on top of the pork.

2. Cover the container and leave it in a cool place for a week.

3. After 1 week, rinse off the salt and dry the pork. Store in a tightly sealed container or wrap tightly in plastic wrap.

4. Before cooking, rinse off any leftover salt (purge the salt). Soak in cold water, rinse well, and pat dry.

*John Steinbeck· *The Grapes of Wrath* (New York): Steinbeck Centennial Edition, 1992, p. 105.

POACHED SAUSAGE

POACHED SAUSAGE
OVER SALT PORK AND LENTILS WITH KALE
COOKED

Yield: 2 servings

SPECIAL TOOLS

Pot for lentils

Pot for poaching

Skillet for searing sausage
 (optional)

INGREDIENTS

½ lb (227 g) salt pork

1 yellow or white onion, cut in half,
 sliced thinly

3–4 cloves garlic (chopped)

1 bay leaf

1 cup (237 ml) French green lentils

4 cups (946 ml) chicken stock (or
 stock of your choice)

1 quart (0.95 l) water (for poaching
 sausage)

2 fresh sausages of your choice

1 bunch kale

WINE PAIRING

Pair with a macerated white wine
or a medium-bodied red blend.

This is one of my favorite comfort foods on a cold winter day. It's incredibly delicious, easy to make, full of nutrients, and supremely warming. Serve it alongside a stiff drink and perhaps a toasty baguette, and let your mind run free.

START WITH THE LENTILS

1. Over medium heat, let the fat from the salt pork render out for about 5 minutes.

2. Add the onions, garlic, and bay leaf, and let brown.

3. Mix in the lentils, stirring occasionally for 3 minutes.

4. Add the stock and stir, making sure to incorporate any bits stuck to the bottom into the stock.

5. Bring to a boil, then cover and lower to a simmer. Let simmer until the lentils are tender.

NOW FOR THE SAUSAGE

1. Bring a quart (0.95 l) of water to a boil.

2. Add the sausages, cover, and turn off the flame. Let sit, covered, for 20 minutes.

NOW FOR THE FINISH

1. Put a cast-iron skillet on the stove over a high flame, and allow the skillet to heat up.

2. When the pan is hot, remove the sausages from the water and give them a quick sear on both sides, until they get a nice brown color. Remove from the pan and set aside.

3. Chop the kale and stir it into the lentils (the idea is to stir in the kale at the end to keep it from overcooking).

4. Serve by making a bed of kale and lentils, and serving the sausage over it.

LARDO
CURED FATBACK: THE POOR MAN'S PROSCIUTTO

CURED

Yield: 8 pieces, ready to be sliced

SPECIAL TOOLS

Pyrex, ceramic, or terra-cotta
  container and cover
A weight for the meat

INGREDIENTS

Sea salt
A solid piece of back fat, cut into
  8" (20 cm) pieces, at least 1" (2.5 cm)
  thick—the thicker the better
Rosemary leaves, removed from
  the sprigs

Some of the most famous lardo in the world comes from a place in Italy called Colonatta. Lardo is traditionally cured in marble vats inside caves for many months at a time. If you have a cave and a marble vat, awesome! You'll be able to make great lardo and I want to try some. If not, have no fear. You'll still be able to make great lardo.

The quality of the fat here is essential. No matter how sharp your technique is, the quality of your lardo will be severely restricted by your ability to source high-quality fat. One reliable way to find quality meat is to head to the farmers' market and ask for the thickest, creamiest, most delicious fatback they've got. For me, heritage-breed pigs produce the best fat, my favorite being the Gloucestershire old spot. Its fat is thick, pure, creamy, and incredibly flavorful.

You can really go to town in terms of adding spices to your lardo. Great-quality fat offers so much pure flavor that I highly encourage you to keep your seasonings simple. Here, we're using two seasonings—salt and rosemary.

1. Massage the sea salt into the fat.

2. Stack pieces of fat on top of each other. Stacks of 2 are enough, but you can stack the fat as high as you'd like. Place the rosemary leaves all along the surfaces of the fat pieces, ensuring even distribution.

3. Place in a Pyrex, ceramic, or terra-cotta container and cover with a piece of parchment paper. Place a weight over the paper, so that the fat is weighed down.

4. After 4 weeks, remove the weight. Let the fat rest in the cooler for at least 3 to 6 months. The famous lardo di Colonnata is rumored to rest in the marble vats for 6 months before being eaten.

5. Slice thin and eat, ideally on warm bread.

LARDO

QUICK PÂTÉ
PREPARED IN BANANA LEAVES
COOKED

Yield: Three 8" (20 cm) pâtés

SPECIAL TOOLS
Meat grinder
Twine
Steamer

INGREDIENTS
1 onion, chopped finely

4 cloves garlic, chopped finely

2 oz (57 g) day-old bread, crust
removed and cut into ½–1"
(13–26 mm) cubes (best to use a
rustic peasant bread)

1 cup (237 ml) red wine

1 lb (454 g) pork belly

2 lbs (1 kg) lean pork shoulder

3 oz (85 g) parsley, chopped

2 oz (57 g) Cognac

¾ oz (21 g) salt

1 oz (28 g) four-spice powder (equal
parts nutmeg, cloves, ginger, pepper)

1 egg

6 banana leaves, cut into 10"
(25.5 cm) long pieces (you can
substitute parchment if banana
leaves are not available)

Bacon or lardo, sliced thinly

Olive oil for sautéing

WINE PAIRING

Pair with a light-bodied red,
such as Beaujolais.

There are so many ways to approach pâté—coarsely chopped, finely ground, spreadable, sliceable, steamed, baked, duck, chicken, pork. The list goes on and on. A pâté is a simple mixture of ground meat, bound together with a binding ingredient (such as eggs and flour), spiced, contained somehow (such as in a mold), and cooked. Here, we will shed light on this highly versatile and world-renowned food using a process that is often seen in tropical regions and employs the banana leaf, an abundant resource that can do a whole lot more than look pretty on the banana plant.

1. Sauté the onions and garlic in olive oil and set aside to cool.

2. Soak the bread in the wine for 15 minutes.

3. While the bread is soaking, prepare the meats by cutting them into cubes, making sure to keep them as cold as possible. Set aside.

4. Remove the bread from the wine, and run the meat and bread through the grinder together, using a ¼" (6 mm) grinding plate. (You can do this by hand, but the grinder is a great help and makes the process much more efficient. Without a grinder, simply chop the meat and bread together until pieces reach a ¼" [6 mm] diameter.)

5. Combine the meat with the onions, garlic, parsley, Cognac, salt, and four-spice. Mix by hand until ingredients are well-incorporated. Let the mixture rest in the refrigerator at least 1 hour, ideally overnight.

6. After the mixture has rested, beat the egg. Remove the meat from the refrigerator and mix the egg into the meat mixture until well-incorporated.

7. Prepare the banana leaves by running them gently over a low flame, back and forth, taking care not to burn them. This will make the banana leaves flexible and prevent them from breaking when assembling the pâtés.

8. Cut the banana leaves into six 10" (25.5 cm) long pieces.

9. Prepare for rolling. Use 2 leaf strips per serving, overlapping one over the other to make sure there is enough leaf to cover the meat.

10. Layer the thinly sliced bacon or lardo down the length of the leaves.

11. Divide the ground meat mixture evenly across the 3 banana leaf wraps, layering it over the bacon or lardo, and roll the leaves shut lengthwise, creating 3 even, uniform "logs."

12. Truss the prepared pâtés by tying a loop at each end to enclose each one, and knotting 5 loops down the length of the pâté to secure it. Let them rest in the refrigerator overnight.

13. After allowing them to rest, steam pâtés for 45 minutes to an hour.

14. Remove the pâtés from the steamer, let them cool, slice them, and serve. Once chilled, these can also be cut into slices and pan-seared.

GRAVLOX

SABLE

COD-LOX

MOJAMA

BUILDING THE SEAFOOD BOARD

Catch your guests off guard at your next gathering! Surprise pescatarian friends, or arouse childhood nostalgia from those who grew up eating cured delights such as sable and lox. As is the story with boards, you can explore many different themes and directions. When working with seafood there are certain components that work really well, and some that are less successful. When arranging accompaniments, I'd think lighter, acidic, and more vegetal. Pickles and fresh salad greens, for example, are great. Onions, carrots, ramps, turnips, radishes, beets, green mangoes, green papaya, and parsnips would all fit beautifully on this board.

SERVES 8-10 PEOPLE

INGREDIENTS

- 4 OZ SALMON LOX, THINLY SLICED ON A BIAS (SEE PAGE 138)

- 4 OZ MOJAMA, THINLY SLICED (SEE PAGE 141)

- 4 OZ "COD-LOX," THINLY SLICED ON A BIAS (SEE PAGE 145)

- 5 OZ SABLE, SLICED ON A BIAS TO 1/3 INCH THICKNESS (SEE PAGE 147)

- 5 OZ DRY-CURED OCTOPUS (SEE PAGE 157) (SOAKED BRIEFLY, DRIED, GRILLED, SLICED ON A BIAS, AND TOSSED IN LEMON)

- 1/2 RED ONION (HALVED AND SLICED THINLY)

- 2 LEMONS

- 1 CUP FRESH PEA SHOOTS

- 3 TEASPOONS OLIVE OIL

- 1 TEASPOON PICKLING LIQUID FROM ONIONS

- 1 CUP CAPERS

- 1 CUP TANGERINE/FIG MOSTARDA (RECIPE ABOVE)

- 1 CUP TOASTED CORN KERNELS

- 2 CLASSIC BAGUETTES (SLICED INTO 1/2 ROUNDS)

- OLIVE OIL FOR BREAD

- SEA SALT

SPECIAL TOOLS

- LARGE SERVING PLATTER (CAN BE A PLATTER, BOARD, SLATE, ETC.)

- SHARP SLICING KNIFE

- 4 RAMEKINS OR MASON JARS FOR PICKLED VEGGIES

- PASTRY BRUSH

INSTRUCTIONS

1. PREHEAT THE OVEN TO 375 DEGREES FAHRENHEIT.

2. DO A QUICK PICKLE OF THE ONIONS BY PLACING THE SLICED ONION INTO A CONTAINER WITH A COVER. SQUEEZE IN THE JUICE OF 1 FRESH LEMON OVER THE ONION AND ADD A PINCH OF SALT. COVER CONTAINER AND SHAKE WELL TO MAKE SURE THE LEMON COATS THE ONIONS. SET ASIDE FOR 1 HOUR.

3. COVER THE DRIED OCTOPUS WITH WATER TO BRIEFLY SOAK. SET ASIDE.

4. BRUSH THE SLICES OF BREAD WITH OLIVE OIL AND SPRINKLE WITH SALT TO TASTE. BAKE UNTIL BREAD BEGINS TO BROWN. SET ASIDE FOR PLATING.

5. REMOVE OCTOPUS FROM WATER AND GRILL OVER MEDIUM HEAT, ALLOWING OCTOPUS TO WARM AND GRILL MARKS TO FORM. REMOVE FROM GRILL, SLICE ON A BIAS, AND TOSS WITH JUICE OF ONE LEMON.

6. ARRANGE ALL THE CURED SEAFOOD OVER HALF OF YOUR PLATTER, PILING AS VOLUMINOUSLY AS POSSIBLE (TRY TO AVOID MAKING THEM LOOK FLAT ON THE PLATE).

7. WHEN THE ONIONS ARE DONE PICKLING, REMOVE 1 TEASPOON OF THE PICKLING BRINE FROM THEIR CONTAINER AND WHISK WITH 3 TEASPOONS OLIVE OIL. TOSS THE PEA SHOOTS IN THIS DRESSING.

8. ARRANGE THE DRESSED PEA SHOOTS ACROSS THE CENTER LINE OF THE PLATTER. PLACE THE PICKLED ONIONS, CAPERS, MUSTARD, AND PRESERVES IN RAMEKINS, AND LINE THEM UP BESIDE THE PEA SHOOTS.

9. PILE THE TOASTS ON THE REMAINING PORTION OF THE PLATTER.

CREATURES OF THE SEA: A BUYER'S GUIDE

If you are lucky enough to have a local fishmonger, by all means, get to know them. Knowing and trusting your local fish supplier is invaluable. If you are lucky enough to be able to fish for yourself, that's even better! The goal should always be achieving the freshest seafood possible.

There's so much that can be said about buying seafood—where it should come from, how to determine freshness, which species are most sustainable, wild-caught vs. farmed, etc. I look to follow two basic rules of thumb when sourcing seafood:

The Fresher the Better

Buying fresh seafood, especially for the purposes of dry-curing, is vital. Seafood that is not fresh runs the risk of not tasting right and making you sick. While I don't always agree that local is better, when it comes to seafood, species that live near to your home will almost always be the freshest available option. If you are lucky enough to have a local fish-monger, by all means, get to know them. They are a wonderful source of knowledge and can teach you about seafood that is local to your area.

It's not always possible to find seafood indigenous to your hometown. When shopping for fish that might have traveled a distance, favor shiny scales over matte appearances and try to find seafood with little to no odor. When purchasing a whole fish, the fish's eyes should be totally clear.

Wild-Caught Over-Farmed

While there are certainly farms raising seafood in a sustainable manner, "farm-raised" seafood is rarely accompanied by information about the raising practices of the farm. Seafood farms, much like livestock farms, are known for intense overcrowding, disease, frequent overuse of antibiotics, poor quality feed, and feed not intended for seafood (i.e. corn for salmon). While there are also concerns to look out for regarding wild-caught seafood, I'd say a general rule of thumb is to buy wild-caught. The exception to this rule would be if you can find information about the conditions and practices of a specific farm, and feel comfortable purchasing their product. There are also apps you can download on a smartphone which serve as useful references when you're headed to the fish market, informing you about local, seasonal seafood, and farming practices for certain breeds of fish.

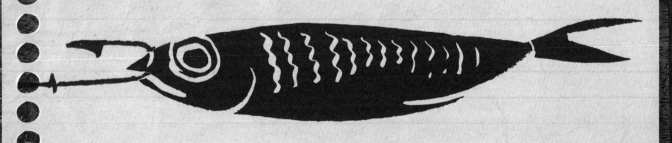

GRAVLOX
CURED

Yield: Approximately 2 lbs (1 kg)

SPECIAL TOOLS

Open container with a flat bottom
  (i.e., Pyrex or hotel pan)
Plastic wrap
A weight for the fish

INGREDIENTS

2½ lbs (1.1 kg) of very fresh wild
  salmon, bones removed
½ shot of bourbon (optional)
Sea salt (1 ½ oz [43 g] per pound
  [454 g] of fish)
Natural cane sugar (Sucanat™,
  if you can find it—Sucanat is
  crystallized sugarcane juice,
  and is one of the purest forms of
  sugar) (½ oz [14 g] per pound of
  fish, about 1 ¼ oz [35 g])
10–15 sprigs dill

Not to be confused with "smoked salmon," gravlox refers to salmon that has been cured. Smoked salmon has been listed on menus as "lox" far too often. True lox is cured simply in a mixture of salt and sugar, and whatever other spice or flavor component the chef uses to bring out the desired taste. Traditionally, lox can be found behind Jewish deli counters, adorned with dill. I prefer lox to be spiced as simply as possible with pure sea salt and super-fresh wild salmon, so that the fatty, buttery flavor of the salmon really shines. The active preparation can be done in under 20 minutes, and is essentially just covering the salmon with the right amount of salt cure.

1. Lay the salmon in an open container with a flat bottom, over a large piece of plastic wrap, skin side down.

2. Gently massage the bourbon into the salmon (optional).

3. Mix together salt and sugar. Gently massage the salt and sugar mixture onto the salmon, taking care to cover all of the salmon, including any crevices.

4. Arrange dill over the salmon. Use enough to dress the entire side of salmon with a "web" of dill. A dense "blanket" of dill would be too much. You should be able to see the salmon through the dill.

5. Tightly wrap the salmon with plastic wrap and leave it on the pan, or in a container with walls. Moisture will be pulled out of the salmon, so if you use a flat cookie sheet or a board, you'll wind up with salmon juice in your refrigerator.

6. Place a weight on top of the salmon (I use a Pyrex baking dish filled with a couple of cans; you can also use a sheet pan with cans, or anything heavy), weighing it down. The salmon should be under a weight during curing.

7. Let the salmon cure in the refrigerator for 48 to 72 hours.

8. When you're ready to eat it, slice the salmon thinly and enjoy. Lox is delicious with a bagel, a chickpea crisp (see the recipe for "Chickpea Flatbread and Lox," page 140), or on its own!

GRAVLOX

CHICKPEA FLATBREAD
WITH LOX, MUSTARD, AND DILL
COOKED

Yield: One 8" (20cm) flatbread (about 4 small servings)

SPECIAL TOOLS

8" (20 cm) cast-iron skillet
  or nonstick pan

INGREDIENTS

½ cup (118 ml) chickpea flour
Pinch salt
½ cup (118 ml) water
2 tablespoons (30 ml) olive oil
  (enough to comfortably fry in)
A thin coating of whole-grain
  mustard for the flatbread
6 slices of lox (see recipe on page 145)
¼ cup (59 ml) capers
¼ red onion, diced
Dill sprigs (for garnish)

WINE PAIRING

Pair with an unoaked crisp white,
such as Chardonnay or Chenin
Blanc, or a sparkling wine, such as
Cava, Crémant, or Prosecco.

Farinata, as this crispy flatbread is also known, is made with chickpea flour and water as its base. You can add salt and spices for flavor. It is deceptively simple and incredibly versatile. This dish is a variation on "bagels and lox," one of the great contributions of Jewish delis to the global food landscape.

1. Slowly incorporate the dry ingredients into the wet ingredients by adding chickpea flour and salt into the water and olive oil, stirring well, making sure there are no lumps. The batter should be slightly thick, about the consistency of tomato juice.

2. Pour a layer of batter into a hot, well-oiled, cast-iron skillet or a nonstick pan, using just enough to cover the whole surface of the pan.

3. Making sure the flatbread is not sticking to the pan, let it cook until the side of the pancake touching the pan is golden brown and crispy.

4. Once it's golden brown and crispy, flip the flatbread and let it cook on the other side until that's also golden brown and crispy.

5. Serve warm. Spread mustard on the flatbread, and top with the lox, capers, onions, and dill sprigs. Cut into 4 wedges and serve.

MOJAMA
(DRY-CURED TUNA LOIN)
CURED

Yield: About 1½ lbs (680g)

SPECIAL TOOLS

Open container with a flat bottom
  (i.e., Pyrex or hotel pan)
A weight for the fish
A hook for hanging

INGREDIENTS

Sea salt to cover, about ½ cup
  (118 ml)
2-lb (1 kg) piece of very fresh side
  of tuna (i.e., loin)

I was lucky enough to be browsing around the Mercado Central in Valencia, Spain, when I casually happened upon mojama at one of the market's smaller stalls. Thank you to the memorable lady in her 60s who took the time to explain to me what was going on in her booth. Salted, air-dried tuna, or the "dry-cured ham of the sea," is a most impressive, delicious, and worthwhile delicacy. You can add this to your list of things to make when those nonpork-eating friends or relatives come over. As with most recipes, freshness and good-quality salt are key. This recipe is so simple that it might make you wonder, as I did, "Why didn't I think of that?" Mojama is delicious sliced thinly and served with sweet melon, wrapped around breadsticks, or served on toasts, with a drizzle of olive oil. It is also wonderful atop a green salad.

1. Make a layer of salt in an open container with a flat bottom (it's best to use Pyrex or a hotel pan). Place the tuna on top of the salt, and cover it with another layer of salt.

2. Place a weight on top of the salt (I use an iron skillet with two or three cans in it). Let the tuna rest for 48 hours in the refrigerator.

3. After 2 days, remove the tuna from the salt and wrap it in a clean, damp cloth. Let it rest in the cloth for 2 more days in the refrigerator. This will help purge the tuna of excess salt.

4. Once 2 days in the cloth have passed, remove the tuna from the cloth.

5. Use a knife to create a hole at the top of the tuna loin, insert a hook, and hang the tuna in a cool place (the refrigerator will work) for 15–20 days, or until sufficiently dry.

CHICKPEA FLATBREAD, page 140

COD-LOX
(DRY-CURED COD)
CURED

Yield: About ¾ lb (340 g) dry-cured cod

SPECIAL TOOLS

Open container with a flat bottom
  (i.e., Pyrex or hotel pan)
A weight for the fish

INGREDIENTS

1 lb (454 g) very fresh wild cod,
  skin on, bones removed
½ shot of Madeira or port wine
1 oz (28 g) sea salt
½ oz (14 g) natural cane sugar
  per 1 lb (454 g) of fish (Sucanat,
  if you can find it)
About 12–15 sprigs parsley or dill
Handful of mint

Sticky and a bit fishy, this is a spin-off of the classic salmon lox. It adds another dimension to your breakfast platter, and offers a way to transform a commonly eaten fish. I'd eat this with something acidic, like lemon juice, and something sweet, like honey. If you're feeling adventurous, use the ingredients in this recipe, and follow the steps to make Mojama, page 141.

1. Lay the cod on a flat-bottom pan, over a large piece of plastic wrap, skin side down.

2. Gently massage the wine into the cod.

3. Mix together salt and sugar. Rub the salt and sugar mixture onto the cod, taking care to cover all of the cod.

4. Arrange herbs over the cod once the cure has been applied. Make sure to dress the entire side of the cod with a "web" of parsley rather than a "blanket." You should be able to see the fish through the parsley.

5. Tightly wrap the cod and leave it on the flat-bottom pan, or in a container with walls. The fish will leech out moisture, so if you use a flat cookie sheet or a board, you'll wind up with cod juice in your refrigerator.

6. Place a weight on top of the cod (I use a cast-iron skillet with some cans—you can also use a sheet pan with cans, or anything heavy). The cod should be under a weight during curing. Let it cure in the refrigerator for 72 hours, checking to make sure the cure is evenly distributed.

7. Slice very thinly and serve over fresh crackers or toasted, thinly sliced bread.

SMOKED SABLE

SMOKED SABLE

CURED

Yield: 2–2½ lbs (1–1.1 kg) smoked sable

SPECIAL TOOLS

Open container with a flat bottom
(i.e., Pyrex or hotel pan)
A smoker (a home oven on low
heat—200-225°F [93-107°C]—
can also be used)

INGREDIENTS

4 oz (113 g) sea salt
1 oz (28 g) pure cane sugar
Three 1-lb (454 g) black cod fillets,
skin on (not to be confused with
cod, which is different)
1 cup (237 ml) honey
Paprika for dusting

Growing up, I lived across the street from a market with a fully stocked smoked fish counter, and sable was among the offerings. Ever-so-slightly sweet, salty, and supremely delicate, sable is a delicacy in every sense of the word. It must be treated with extreme care, especially when slicing, or it will break apart. Sable is a must for the Jewish-style deli counter enthusiast. It's great with a bagel. But before you start eating it with other things, get to know the nuances of this dish on its own. Taste it, savor it, and make enough for seconds.

1. Mix salt and sugar and gently massage the mixture into the fish. Place the fish, skin side down, into a plastic wrap–covered container. Wrap tightly and leave in the refrigerator overnight to cure.

2. After the overnight cure, remove the fish from the wrap and rinse with cold water.

3. Prepare your smoker, using the wood of your choice. Bring the temperature of the smoker to 175°F (79°C) degrees.

4. Brush each fillet with honey. Place a piece of parchment paper (or aluminum foil) under each fillet and smoke for approximately 2½ hours, brushing with honey again after 2 hours.

5. Remove the fish from the smoker and let it cool, removing the pin bones that run down to middle of the fish with tweezers. The bones should slide right out once the fish is cooked.

6. Dust with paprika, and slice with tremendous care, on a bias.

BOTARGO
(DRY-CURED FISH ROE)
CURED

Yield: 2 pieces botargo

SPECIAL TOOLS

Flat-bottomed container
  (i.e., a Pyrex pan)
A weight (a skillet, a brick, or a
  bacon press work well)
Netting or cheesecloth for hanging

INGREDIENTS

2 fish roe (can be shad, sea bass,
  mackerel, or the fish that is
  freshest in your area)
1 cup (237 ml) sea salt

If ever there were a canon of delicacies in the world of dry-cured creatures of the sea, botargo would be among the names listed. It can be made with a wide variety of roe, including tuna, shad, sea bass, and mullet. In this recipe, I use roe from the sea bass, as it is the freshest in the area where I live. That said, you can substitute, depending on what's fresh and available in your area. Botargo is an amazing ingredient to have around, it's easy to make, and it can be quite inexpensive as well. Salty, umami, and reminiscent of the ocean, this delicacy can be grated over pasta, folded into sauces, or sliced thinly on a baguette. Use sparingly, as a little will go a long way.

1. Rinse roe and pat dry.

2. In a flat-bottomed container, spread a layer of salt to a thickness of about 1/8" (3 mm). Layer the roe over the salt and cover the rest of the roe with another 1/8" (3 mm) layer of salt. Lay parchment paper over the fish and set the weight on top of the roe. Let it sit in the refrigerator for about 10 hours.

3. After 10 hours, remove the roe from the salt and rinse under cold water to remove the salt.

4. Wrap the roe in a thin layer of cheesecloth or in netting and let it dry for 10–14 days in a cool place, making sure there is some humidity to keep the roe from getting too dry. You can do this in the refrigerator, but I recommend putting an uncovered bowl of salted water on the same shelf to create humidity (salt will keep bacteria from growing in the water).

BOTARGO

CRISPY RICE CREPE
WITH BOTARGO AND HEARTY GREEN SALAD
COOKED

Yield: 2 pancakes

SPECIAL TOOLS
Nonstick skillet

INGREDIENTS

For Pancakes

1 cup (237 ml) white rice flour (you can substitute brown rice flour, depending on your preference)

1 cup (237 ml) water

½ cup (118 ml) coconut milk

½ oz (14 g) botargo (see recipe page 149), grated

For Salad

3 cups (710 ml) kale, chopped

½ cup (118 ml) radicchio, chopped

½ cup (118 ml) mint leaves

1 cup (237 ml) raw almonds, toasted and coarsely chopped

1 teaspoon (5 ml) whole-grain mustard

1 tablespoon (15 ml) fresh lemon juice

1 teaspoon (5 ml) rice vinegar

½ teaspoon (2.5 ml) honey

3 tablespoons (45 ml) olive oil

WINE PAIRING

Pair with a macerated white or an aromatic white, such as Sauvignon Blanc or Trebbiano.

This is a variation of a traditional Vietnamese pancake. You can get creative with the batter, throwing in spices, textural elements, and flavoring elements. I love to add a little bit of coconut milk to the batter. It doesn't take long to put this dish together, and it can be great shared or as an individual portion. Miniature versions of this recipe are a delicious finger food. If you want, you can swap the salad for a slice of vegetable (i.e., beet, carrot, radish), or a nice slice of fresh sausage. The sky is really the limit here, so let your imagination run free!

1. Make rice milk by whisking together rice flour, water, and coconut milk until smooth (this can also be done in a blender).

2. After these ingredients are well-incorporated, whisk in grated botargo. Let the mixture rest for at least 30 minutes.

3. While the rice milk is sitting, chop kale, radicchio, and mint and combine.

4. Toast almonds on stovetop until they begin to brown and become fragrant. Coarsely chop and set aside.

5. Make vinaigrette by whisking together the mustard, lemon juice, rice vinegar, and honey. Once combined, drizzle in olive oil, whisking continuously.

6. Heat the skillet, coating with enough oil to keep the pancake from sticking (about 2 tablespoons [30 ml]). After a minute or less, you will see wisps of smoke. Then, pour in half the rice pancake batter. When the downward-facing side of the pancake is golden brown and crispy, flip and cook the other side in the same way. Set the pancake aside.

7. Combine the chopped greens and toasted almonds. Dress with the vinaigrette to your liking.

8. Plate either open face, with the salad in the middle of the pancake, or arrange the salad on one half of the pancake and fold the other half over it.

HOMEMADE MATZO
WITH SABLE, HORSERADISH, AND PARSLEY
COOKED

Yield: 5 open-face matzo sandwiches

SPECIAL TOOLS
Rolling pin
Baking sheet or baking stone (I prefer a baking stone)
Food processor

INGREDIENTS

For Matzo
1 cup (237 ml) all-purpose flour
1 cup (237 ml) whole-wheat flour
¾ cup (177 ml) cold water + more as needed

For Horseradish
1 lb (454 g) fresh horseradish root, peeled and cut into cubes
2 tablespoons (30 ml) white or cider vinegar

For Topping
8 oz (227 g) sable (see recipe for "Smoked Sable," page 147)
5 sprigs parsley (for garnish)

WINE PAIRING

Pair with a light-red wine, such as Beaujolais, or a light, crisp white, such as Viognier or unoaked Chardonnay.

By definition, matzo is a quick food. Legend has it that matzo, an unleavened crisp, was originally made by Jewish people fleeing persecution in the deserts of Egypt. It is essentially bread without yeast, because when you're on the run, there's no time to wait for bread to rise. Moreover, it was baked to a crispy texture, devoid of moisture, to aid in preservation. All that said, why is matzo so rarely made at home? Where does the complacency with the store-bought variety of this culturally rich, highly useful, and invariably versatile food stem from? While there is surely a loaded answer to this question, there is no time like the present to try one's luck with making matzo at home. And once you've done that, adorn it with sable, the golden child of Jewish smoked fish, and a touch of homemade horseradish. It will clear your sinuses and soothe your soul, all in one luscious bite.

FOR MATZO

1. Preheat the oven to 425°F (218°C), with the baking sheet or baking stone inside.

2. Combine flours and water and knead for about 5 minutes until the dough is uniform.

3. Divide dough into 5 pieces. Roll each piece out until about 1/8" (3 mm) thick.

4. Use a fork to prick neat rows across the matzos. This will keep bubbles from forming while the matzos are baking.

5. Bake the matzos on the preheated sheet or stone until golden brown.

6. Let cool on a rack.

FOR HORSERADISH

1. Peel the horseradish root with a sharp knife or a potato peeler and cut the root into cubes. Pulse in food processor until finely grated.

2. Set aside for 10 minutes, then add the vinegar and pulse until well-incorporated.

3. Seal in a mason jar.

FOR ASSEMBLY

1. Spread a small dollop of horseradish on each piece of matzo.

2. Carefully slice the sable on a bias and layer on top of the horseradish. Garnish with a sprig of parsley.

ROMANESCO BROCCOLI
WITH BOTARGO, LEMON, AND TOMATO VINAIGRETTE
COOKED

Yield: 3-4 servings

INGREDIENTS

1 head of fresh Romanesco
(broken down into "florets")

4 fresh, medium-sized tomatoes,
finely chopped

1 clove of garlic, chopped

½ oz (2.5 ml) botargo, grated

¼ cup (59 ml) olive oil

Juice from ½ lemon

WINE PAIRING

Pair with a light- to medium-
bodied red, such as Barbera or
Beaujolais.

With its haunting symmetry, exuberant green color, and obelisk-like tops, Romanesco broccoli could hold its own next to any botanical adornment. Its distinguished appearance aside, its flavor is quite mellow, with a mildly discernible nuttiness reminiscent of cauliflower and broccoli. Lightly poach it with some well-thought-out flavoring elements and you have yourself a standout side dish or an ideal accompaniment to be tossed with pasta. Peak season for Romanesco is late in the summer, just as fall is arriving.

1. In well-salted, boiling water, poach the Romanesco for 3 minutes. Drain and set aside.

2. Cook the tomatoes, garlic, botargo, and 1 tablespoon (15 ml) of olive oil in a saucepan over medium-low heat, stirring often, until the tomatoes are uniform and easily spreadable. This should take 10 to 15 minutes. Make sure the botargo has dissolved.

3. Squeeze the lemon over the tomatoes, stirring constantly, and then drizzle the remaining olive oil, continuing to stir, until the consistency is a little thicker than tomato juice, and slightly thinner than a smoothie. Add more olive oil and/or lemon accordingly. You shouldn't need salt at this point (the botargo is fairly salty), but if you find it needs some, by all means add it.

4. In a bowl, toss the Romanesco in the oil and tomato dressing, making sure all the Romanesco is well-coated. Serve.

ONE-HOUR CURED-FISH APPETIZER

CURED

Yield: 16-20 slices

SPECIAL TOOLS
Large platter

INGREDIENTS
1 lb (454 g) wild salmon
 and/or cod
3 tablespoons (45 ml)
 olive oil
3 tablespoons (45 ml)
 lemon juice
Sea salt

This recipe works well with a variety of fish—whitefish, salmon, bass, tuna. It is extra delicious with salmon.

1. Slice fish very thinly and lay slices on a large platter.
2. Blend olive oil and lemon juice and drizzle over slices of fish.
3. Sprinkle salt over all the slices, making sure that salt is evenly distributed.
4. Let the platter sit in the refrigerator for 1 hour.
5. Serve with bread and/or crackers.

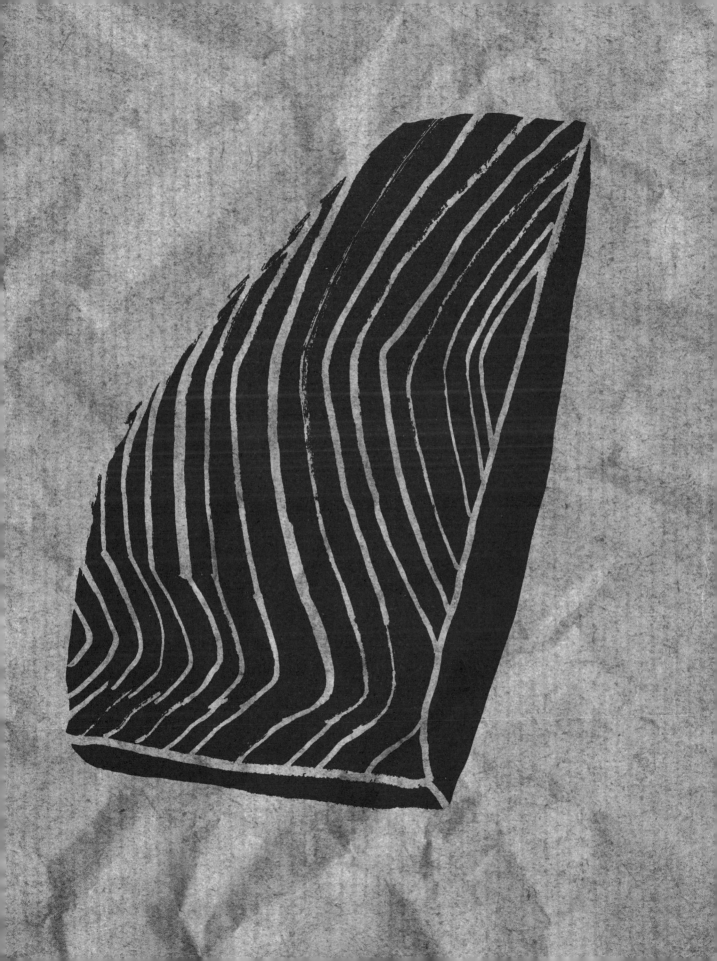

DRY-CURED WHOLE OCTOPUS

DRY-CURED WHOLE OCTOPUS

CURED

Yield: 1 cured octopus

SPECIAL TOOLS

Flat-bottomed container
  or large bowl
A clean, damp cloth

INGREDIENTS

1 whole, very fresh octopus
Sea salt
Good-quality bread
Red onions pickled in
  lemon juice and mint

This distinct preservation of octopus has been prepared for years in Spain and Greece. It is a way to preserve a freshly-caught octopus, and helps to transform its flavor and texture. If you perform a web search for "pulpo seco" (dried octopus), a variety of incredible images will display various methods used around the world to prepare dry octopus. Once cured, I would recommend finishing the octopus on the grill or poaching and serving very simply, with a high-quality olive oil.

1. Rinse the octopus well.

2. Make a layer of salt on the bottom of a flat-bottomed container or a large bowl. Put the octopus on top of the salt, and coat with salt, making sure the salt is penetrating the entire octopus. (Because of the shape of the octopus, it is easy to miss some areas of the octopus, even if appears to be completely covered in salt. Make sure every part is covered.) Cover and let it rest in the refrigerator for 24 hours.

3. After the 24-hour rest period, remove the octopus from the salt and wrap it in a damp cloth. Leave the octopus to purge for 1 day in the refrigerator.

4. Spread the legs of the octopus apart and hang it in a cool place (the refrigerator will work) for 10–14 days, making sure the legs and head are not touching each other.

5. When you're ready to serve the octopus, grill or sauté it on each side until it's seared. Serve it sliced with good bread, and garnish with red onions pickled in lemon juice and mint.

PANIPURI
WITH DRY-CURED OCTOPUS, FAVA BEAN PURÉE, AND DICED FIG
COOKED

Yield: About 10 pieces

SPECIAL TOOLS
Skillet for frying

Rolling pin

1½" (4 cm) round cookie cutter

INGREDIENTS

For Bread

½ cup (118 ml) semolina flour

¼ cup (59 ml) warm water

2 teaspoons (10 ml) all-purpose flour

Pinch of salt

Oil for frying

For Filling

4 oz (113 g) fresh fava beans, boiled and shelled (4 oz [113 g] after boiling and shelling)

Salt to taste

2 tablespoons (30 ml) olive oil, plus more for drizzling

Juice from 1 lemon

4 oz (113 g) dry-cured octopus, poached for 5 minutes and sliced thinly

4 dried figs

WINE PAIRING

Pair with a medium- to full-bodied red, such as Pinot Noir or Syrah, or a medium-bodied white, such as Chardonnay.

This dish is a great social lubricant—it is made in individual servings and doesn't require divvying up at the table. I couldn't include this recipe without a tip of the hat to its homeland of India. Panipuri is a miniature version of the deep-fried, puffy bread called bhatoora. It can be opened up, creating a hollow to be filled with a wide range of tasty condiments. This version of panipuri hits the three textural elements—crunchy, springy, and soft—along with the three flavor elements—savory, sour, and sweet.

FOR BREAD

1. Place the semolina flour into a bowl, and massage half the water into the flour until well-incorporated. Flour should be uniformly damp. Let it rest for 5 minutes.

2. Add in the all-purpose flour and salt and knead well for at least 5 minutes, until the dough is soft and smooth.

3. Let it rest for 30 minutes to an hour.

4. After the dough has rested, roll out the dough as thinly as possible without it breaking it (about 1/8" [3 mm]). Using the cookie cutter, cut out 1½" (4 cm) rounds.

5. Heat the oil in a skillet and fry rounds of dough in the hot oil (between 350°F and 400°F [177–204°C]). The dough should puff up when it hits the oil. If it doesn't, your oil is not hot enough. If your oil smokes, it is too hot.

6. Fry little breads on both sides until golden brown. Set aside on a paper towel–covered wire rack to absorb the oil and allow the breads to cool. If you cool them on a solid, flat surface, they'll get soft on the bottom. Airflow is essential.

FOR FILLING

1. Boil the fava beans in salted water until tender. Drain and peel.

2. Combine the olive oil, salt, and juice from half of the lemon with the favas and mash using a fork or a hand potato masher until you have a purée. Set aside.

3. Poach the octopus for 5 minutes and slice as thinly as possible, making sure to cut enough for 1–2 slices per bread. Toss with the juice of the other half of the lemon. Set aside.

4. Remove stems from dry figs and dice finely. Set aside.

FOR PLATING

1. Remove a small piece from the top of each bread, creating a cup-like hollow. Spoon a dollop of fava purée into each hollow.

2. Spoon 1 or 2 small cubes of diced fig over the purée.

3. Layer the octopus slices over the fava and figs and serve.

PANIPURI, page 158

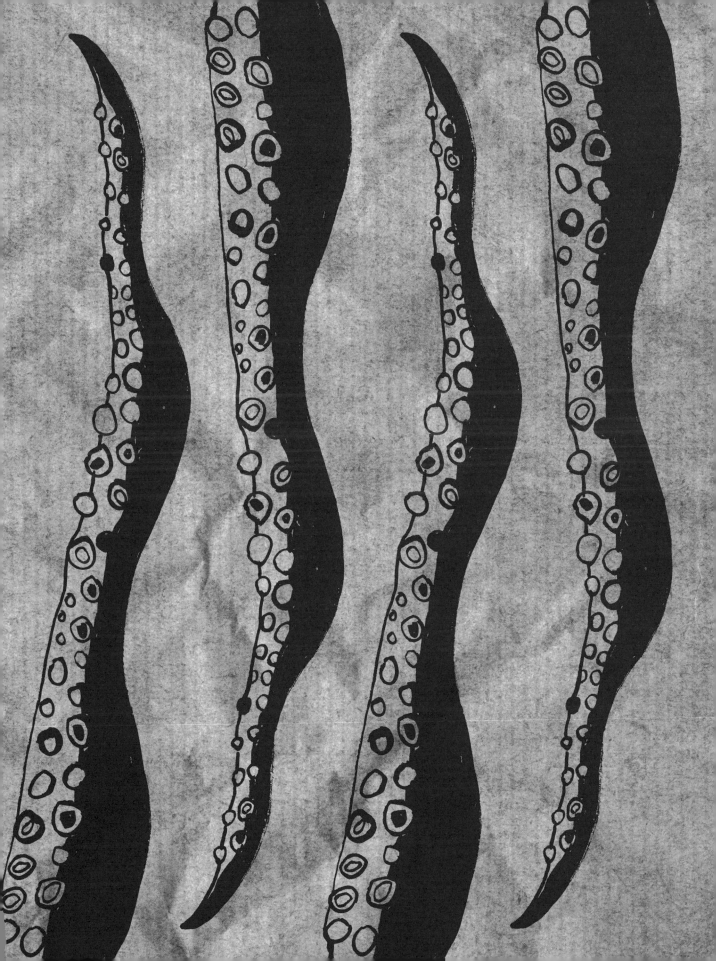

SALTED MELON & CUCUMBER

FIG "SALAMI"

FRUITS & VEGETABLES

CRISPY CHICKPEAS

BEETS IN YOGURT

BUILDING THE VEGETARIAN BOARD

The vegetarian board affords an opportunity to showcase the bounty of the garden. You can really go to town presenting vegetables and fruits in a variety of forms, exploring a multitude of textures and tastes. When I think of a great vegetarian board, I think of something super fresh, that doesn't weigh you down, but leaves you satiated. Avoid the temptation to arrange a board of raw, conventionally cooked fruits and vegetables. Not only is there a valuable utility in serving preserved fruits and veggies, your board will delight vegetarian guests who are otherwise excluded from the charcuterie board. While I firmly believe that this vegetarian board can stand proudly on its own, a great vegetarian board happens to be a sharp accompaniment to a meat board, if your eating habits permit.

The recipe for the board below is full of strong flavors—salty, sweet, salty/sweet, acidic, umami, pungent. It's arranged in the spirit of having to be creative and having to push the envelope when keeping things strictly vegetarian.

SERVES 8-10 PEOPLE

INGREDIENTS

- 5 OZ AIR-DRIED MELON, SLICED (SEE PAGE 181)
- 2 FRESH, CRUNCHY CUCUMBERS, WASHED, HALVED, AND SEEDED
- 10 FRESH BASIL LEAVES
- 5 OZ AIR-DRIED BEETS, SLICED
- 1 CUP PLAIN YOGURT
- 1 CUP CHICKPEAS
- 1/4 CUP CHICKPEA FLOUR
- 1 SMALL HOT CHILI, SEEDS REMOVED AND SLICED THINLY
- OIL FOR FRYING
- 5 OZ AIR-DRIED PERSIMMON, SLICED (SEE PAGE 177)
- 5 OZ SALTED CUCUMBERS, CUBED (SEE PAGE 185)
- 5 OZ FIG "SALAMI," (SEE PAGE 167)
- 5 OZ FALL FRUIT "SALAMI" (SEE PAGE 174)
- 5 OZ DATE "SALAMI" (SEE PAGE 173)
- FOR TOMATO JAM
- 6 TOMATOES, PEELED AND CHOPPED
- OLIVE OIL TO TASTE
- SALT TO TASTE
- FOR MATZO
- 1 CUP ALL-PURPOSE FLOUR
- 1 CUP WHOLE WHEAT FLOUR
- 3/4 CUP + MORE AS NEEDED COLD WATER
- OLIVE OIL FOR DRIZZLING

- 1 WHOLE GRAIN PEASANT BREAD (SLICED ON BIAS)
- 1 CLASSIC BAGUETTE (SLICED INTO ROUNDS)
- 1 RECIPE FOR "MATZO" (RECIPE BELOW) (BROKEN INTO LARGE CHUNKS)

SPECIAL TOOLS

- SERVING PLATTER
- 5 RAMEKINS (OR SMALL MASON JARS)

INSTRUCTIONS

FOR TOMATO JAM

1. COOK THE TOMATOES IN A SAUCEPAN OVER MEDIUM-LOW HEAT, WITH 1 TABLESPOON OF OLIVE OIL, STIRRING OFTEN, UNTIL THE TOMATOES ARE UNIFORM AND EASILY SPREADABLE. THIS SHOULD TAKE 10 TO 15 MINUTES. ADD SALT TO TASTE.

2. PLACE IN A RAMEKIN OR JAR AND SET ASIDE.

FOR MATZO

1. PREHEAT THE OVEN, WITH THE BAKING SHEET OR STONE INSIDE, TO 425 DEGREES FAHRENHEIT.

2. COMBINE FLOUR AND WATER AND KNEAD FOR ABOUT 5 MINUTES UNTIL THE DOUGH IS UNIFORM.

3. DIVIDE DOUGH INTO 5 BALLS.

4. ROLL EACH BALL OUT UNTIL INTO 1/8" THICK ROUNDS.

5. USE A FORK TO PRICK NEAT ROWS ACROSS THE MATZOS. THIS WILL KEEP BUBBLES FROM FORMING WHILE BAKING

6. BAKE THE MATZOS ON THE PREHEATED SHEET OR STONE UNTIL GOLDEN BROWN.

7. LET COOL ON A RACK BEFORE REMOVING FROM OVEN AND SETTING ASIDE.

FOR CHICKPEAS

1. TOSS THE CHICKPEAS IN CHICKPEA FLOUR AND DEEP FRY UNTIL GOLDEN BROWN AND CRISPY.

2. TOSS IN SALT AND CHILI TO TASTE.

3. SERVE IN A RAMEKIN OR JAR.

FOR MELON AND CUCUMBERS

1. FINELY DICE THE MELON. FILL THE SEEDED CUCUMBERS WITH THE MELON.

2. CUT ALONG EACH PIECE OF CUCUMBER, CREATING BITE-SIZED, 1/2 PIECES.

3. TOP WITH CHOPPED FRESH BASIL

FOR BEETS AND YOGURT

1. GRATE OR FINELY DICE BEETS.

2. STIR BEETS INTO PLAIN YOGURT. PLACE INTO REFRIGERATOR AND ALLOW TO REST FOR AT LEAST ONE HOUR.

3. SERVE IN A RAMEKIN OR JAR.

TO ARRANGE BOARD

1. DIVIDE THE BOARD INTO 2 PARTS, ONE SLIGHTLY LARGER THAN THE OTHER.

2. ON THE SMALLER SIDE OF THE BOARD, ARRANGE RAMEKINS FILLED WITH BEET AND YOGURT MIXTURE, FRIED CHICKPEAS, AND TOMATO JAM.

3. ARRANGE THE PRESERVED PERSIMMON AND THE 3 FRUIT SALAMIS ON THE LARGER PART OF THE BOARD. "OPEN" THE FRUIT SALAMIS BY BEGINNING TO SLICE ONE END OF EACH SALAMI, INVITING GUESTS TO DIVE RIGHT IN.

4. ARRANGE THE BREADS IN A BASKET OR ON THEIR OWN PLATTER, SEPARATING THE WHOLE-WHEAT BAGUETTE, CLASSIC BAGUETTE, AND MATZO INTO THREE SEPARATE PILES.

FRUITS & VEGETABLES: A BUYER'S GUIDE

When buying fruits and vegetables for curing, look for produce that is as fresh and flavorful as possible, paying attention to the time of year to shop for fruit in-season. Just because you can buy blueberries or strawberries in New York City in winter doesn't mean you should! Stick with fruits and vegetables that were grown locally for the freshest product. They are more likely to have ripened on the vine or bush, producing a more flavorful product. Fruit that is shipped around the world is often picked prematurely, and encouraged to ripen on store shelves or in your home.

Fruits bearing soft spots, bruises, and indentations are better used for preserved foods like jams, sauces, and reductions. There's no need to throw them away.

DRY-CURED FRUITS AND VEGETABLES

DRY FIG "SALAMI"

CURED

Yield: Approximately fifteen 5-oz (142 g) fig "salamis"

SPECIAL TOOLS

Netting (size #10)
Sausage stuffer

INGREDIENTS

5 lbs (2.3 kg) dry figs (your favorite
 kind—we use black mission)
2 cups (473 ml) red wine
1 cup (237 ml) bourbon
Sea salt to taste
1½" (4 cm) synthetic fibrous
 casings

Fig "salami" is the ultimate accompaniment to a charcuterie or cheese plate, as well as a tasty alternative to your classic jam. It can be sliced or spread, has no added sugar, is naturally sweet, and stores extremely well for long periods of time.

1. De-stem all the figs and run them through a meat grinder. If you don't have a meat grinder, a food processor should work. Otherwise, just chop by hand until they're about the consistency of a paste. Adding a little bit of the liquor at this step will help, as the fruit alone can be quite dense.

2. In a mixer (or with your hands), add the wine, bourbon, and a pinch of sea salt and mix until well-incorporated.

3. Using a sausage stuffer, stuff the fig mixture into the casings, taking care to pinch the casing between each link.

4. Place the "salamis" in the netting and tie off the links, making a loop at the end to hang the fig "salamis." Hang the "salamis" for 3 or 4 days, until they ripen a bit and lose some of their moisture. Because you're not working with meat, spoilage is much less of a concern. I like to hang these next to a partially opened window so they can catch a breeze.

5. Store indefinitely, knowing that the longer you wait to eat these, the drier they'll be and the more concentrated the flavors will become.

QUEENS COUNTY MARKET SANDWICH
CHORIZO, FRESH RICOTTA, FIG "SALAMI," AND ARUGULA ON HOMEMADE CUBAN BREAD

COOKED

Yield: 4 sandwiches

SPECIAL TOOLS
Electric mixer (you can substitute human hands)
Rolling pin
Baking sheet (approximately 13" x 18" [33 x 45.5 cm])

INGREDIENTS

For Bread
1 packet active, dry yeast
2 teaspoons (10 ml) sugar
1¼ cups (296 ml) warm water
2 cups (473 ml) bread flour (you can substitute 2 cups [473 ml] all-purpose flour)
2 cups (473 ml) all-purpose flour
3 teaspoons (15 ml) salt
¼ cup (59 ml) lard

For Filling
1 fig "salami," peeled (you can substitute fig jam if you don't have fig "salami")
8 oz (227 g) fresh ricotta
8 oz (227 g) dry-cured chorizo, sliced
4 handfuls arugula

WINE PAIRING

Pair with a light-red wine, such as Carignan, Grenache, or Pinot Noir.

Out of all the sandwich varieties that we serve at our markets, this is my favorite. We only make it at one market, once a month—the Queens County Market. All the soul packed into this sandwich is compounded when it's done on freshly baked Cuban bread. Take the time to make the Cuban bread at home, if you can. Done right, it will be worth every second of the two or three hours it takes to make. I like this sandwich cold, but you can always take it a step further and give it a press, leaving you with a crunchy exterior and a soft inside.

FOR THE CUBAN BREAD

1. Preheat the oven to 450°F (232°C), with a pan of water in the oven. The pan of water will help create humidity in the oven, which is very beneficial for bread baking.

2. "Wake up" the yeast by mixing together the sugar, ¼ cup (59 ml) of lukewarm water, and the dry yeast. Let the mixture sit for 15 minutes, or until a frothiness develops on the top (like what you'd see in a glass of beer).

3. While the yeast wakes up, sift the flour and salt together in a mixing bowl. Set aside.

4. Heat the lard in a saucepan until just melted. Remove from heat, and add the second cup of lukewarm water to the lard.

5. Add the lard mixture to the yeast mixture and combine.

6. Slowly add the dry ingredients (flour and salt) to the wet ingredients (water, yeast, lard), making sure to stir continuously. Reserve a little bit of flour for rolling out the dough.

7. Knead until the dough is elastic and smooth, about 15 minutes by hand, or 4–5 minutes in an electric mixer outfitted with a dough hook.

8. Once smooth, place the dough into a lightly greased bowl covered with a towel. Let it rise in a dark, room-temperature space for 1 hour.

9. When the dough has risen, roll out the dough to ¾" (2 cm) on a lightly floured surface. Rolled-out dough should be about 12" (30.5 cm) wide by 18" (45.5 cm) long (21" [56.5 cm], or 3" [7.5 cm] less than the diagonal length of your baking sheet).

10. Roll the dough into a tight cylinder. Gently taper the ends by pinching and folding them under to form the loaf.

11. Lay the loaf, seam-side down, on the diagonal of a baking sheet (this will ensure the longest loaf possible). Score the top with a razor blade or a sharp knife, first vertically down the middle of the loaf, then horizontally across the middle of the loaf. You should end up with a scored cross.

12. Loosely cover and leave to rise again in a dark place at around room temperature for about another hour, until your loaf is 2–3 times its original size.

13. Bake for about 15 minutes, or until golden brown.

FOR THE FILLING

1. Slice the bread open, making sure not to slice all the way through, so you can "fold" the sandwich back together.

2. Smear the fig "salami" on the bread.

3. Next spread the ricotta on the bread.

4. Next layer the chorizo.

5. Finally, pack the arugula in the sandwich, fold closed, and serve.

QUEENS COUNTY MARKET SANDWICH, page 168

SHORTCUT GELATO, page 172

SHORTCUT GELATO
WITH FIG AND BASIL
COOKED

Yield: A little more than 1 pint (473 ml) of gelato

INGREDIENTS

1 pint (473 ml) vanilla gelato

1 fig "salami," peeled and softened with a wooden spoon or spatula

A handful of fresh basil, chopped finely

Splash of bourbon

Here's a shortcut if you want to elevate a dessert but have little time to spare. It's the old compounding technique: You can make the gelato yourself, for example, and incorporate the other ingredients accordingly, or simply go ahead and buy a nice pint of classic vanilla ice cream or gelato at your local store. This can go in a variety of directions—add toasted nuts, different fruits, or different liquors, for completely different tastes. Here is the simplest rendition of this recipe.

1. Soften the gelato by setting it out on the counter for 3–4 minutes, or by gently stirring it with a wooden spoon or spatula.

2. Add a little bourbon to the fig "salami" and mash with a wooden spoon to soften.

3. Fold the softened fig "salami" and the chopped basil into the gelato.

4. Return the gelato to its container, place it in the freezer, and allow it to set for at least an hour, but ideally overnight.

DRY DATE "SALAMI"
WITH BLANCHED, SALTED ALMONDS
CURED

Yield: Approximately fifteen 5-oz (142 g) fig "salamis"

SPECIAL TOOLS
Sausage stuffer
Netting (size #10)

INGREDIENTS
¼ cup (118 ml) sea salt
6 cups (1.4 l) water
3 cups (710 ml) raw almonds
5 lbs (2.3 kg) pitted dates
1 cup (473 ml) high-quality gin
1½" (4 cm) synthetic fibrous
   casings

This variation on the fig "salami" is a delicious accompaniment to a charcuterie or cheese plate. Use it like a jam, and store it like a salami.

1. Dissolve salt in boiling water. Allow the water to cool until it is a comfortable temperature to touch (around room temperature). Blanch the almonds in the water overnight, either in your refrigerator or on the counter.

2. After blanching, remove the skins from the almonds and set them aside.

3. Run the dates through a meat grinder. If you don't have a meat grinder, a food processor should work. Otherwise, just chop the dates by hand until they're the consistency of a paste. Adding a little bit of the liquor at this step will help, as the fruit alone can be quite dense.

4. In a mixer (or with your hands), combine the dates, almonds, and gin until well-incorporated. Using a sausage stuffer, stuff the mixture into casings, taking care to pinch the casing between each link.

5. Place the sausages into the netting and tie off the links, making a loop at the end to hang the date "salamis." Hang them in a cool place for 3 or 4 days, until they ripen a bit and lose some of their moisture.

6. Store them indefinitely, knowing the longer you wait to eat these, the drier they'll be and the more concentrated the flavors will become.

FALL FRUIT "SALAMI"

CURED

Yield: Approximately fifteen 5-oz (142 g) fall fruit "salamis"

SPECIAL TOOLS
Sausage stuffer
Netting (size #10)

INGREDIENTS
2½ lbs (1.1 kg) dried apples
2½ lbs (1.1 kg) dried pears
2 cups (473 ml) tart, craft cider
½ cup (118 ml) bourbon
2 cups (473 ml) raw or roasted
  hazelnuts
Salt to taste (about ½ teaspoon
  [2.5 ml])
1½" (4 cm) synthetic fibrous
  casings

This seasonal variation on dry fruit "salami" is perfect to make with the last fruits of fall, just before winter hits. A wonderful complement to cheese and cured meats, this fall "salami" is also delicious on freshly baked or warmed bread.

1. De-stem the apples and pears, and run them through a meat grinder. If you don't have a meat grinder, a food processor should work. Otherwise, just chop the fruit by hand until it forms the consistency of a smooth paste. Adding a little bit of the liquor at this step will help, as the fruit alone can be quite dense.

2. In a mixer (or with your hands), add the cider, bourbon, hazelnuts, and salt to taste, and mix until well-incorporated. Using a sausage stuffer, stuff mixture into casings, taking care to pinch the casing between each link.

3. Place sausages into netting and tie off the links, making a loop at the end to hang the date salamis. Hang them for 3 or 4 days, until they ripen a bit and lose some of their moisture.

4. Store indefinitely, knowing that the longer you wait to eat these, the drier they'll be and the more concentrated the flavors will become.

DRY APRICOT "SALAMI"

CURED

Yield: Approximately fifteen 5-oz (142 g) apricot "salamis"

SPECIAL TOOLS

Sausage stuffer

Netting (size #10)

INGREDIENTS

3 cups (710 ml) toasted walnuts

5 lbs (2.3 kg) unsulfured, dried apricots

1 cup (237 ml) grappa

Salt to taste (approximately ½ teaspoon [2.5 ml])

1½" (4 cm) synthetic fibrous casings

In this fruit "salami," apricots offer a bright, tangy note. Be sure to use unsulfured apricots, as sulfur has been known to cause headaches, and will cause your "salami" to take on a bright, synthetic orange color.

1. Toast the walnuts in an oven set to 350°F (177°C) degrees for 15–20 minutes, or on the stovetop, until browned but not burning. They'll start to release a delicious aroma when they're almost done. Set aside and let cool.

2. Run the apricots through a meat grinder. If you don't have a meat grinder, a food processor should work. Otherwise, just chop the apricots by hand until they're about the consistency of a smooth paste. Adding a little bit of the liquor at this step will help, as the fruit alone can be quite dense.

3. In a mixer (or with your hands), add the grappa, toasted walnuts, and salt to taste, and mix until well-incorporated. Using a sausage stuffer, stuff the mixture into the casings, taking care to pinch the casing between each link.

4. Put in the netting and tie off the links, making a loop at the end to hang the apricot "salamis." Hang them for 3 or 4 days, until they ripen a bit and lose some of their moisture.

5. Store indefinitely, knowing the longer you wait to eat these, the drier they'll be and the more concentrated the flavors will become.

SALT-CURED FRUITS AND VEGETABLES

SALTED, DRIED PERSIMMON FRUIT

CURED

Yield: About 8 persimmons

SPECIAL TOOLS

Container for salting

Skewer

INGREDIENTS

2 lbs (1 kg) fuyu persimmons

4 oz (113 g) sea salt

As with nearly all recipes involving dry-curing, it's worth trying this recipe a few times, and adjusting the salt levels to your taste. Take care to use fuyu persimmons, as they are crunchier and lend themselves better to this recipe. The larger variety, known as hachiya, will leave your mouth feeling numb if they're not eaten when they're extremely ripe and soft. The harder, crunchier texture of the fuyus will yield a more workable texture.

1. Remove persimmon stems and cut fruits into ½" (13 mm) rounds. Place the persimmon slices in a container with salt and cover them.

2. Let the persimmons rest in the salt for at least 24 hours.

3. After 24 hours, rinse off the salt and dry the persimmons. Run the skewer through the persimmon slices and hang them in a cool, drafty place (a rack, refrigerator, or oven with the door propped open) for a week, or until they are dry.

AMARO-SOAKED SALTED PERSIMMON PRESERVES

COOKED

Yield: About 2 cups preserves (473 ml)

INGREDIENTS

4 salted fuyu persimmons

2 cups (237 ml) amaro liqueur

1 tablespoon (15 ml) honey

These are a bit intense to eat on their own, so I'd try them on some shortbread or as a digestif after a meal. They can also be used as a "mouth-waterer" before a meal to start digestion. Expect a punch of sweetness with bitter notes from the amaro.

1. Soak the persimmons in cold water for 30 minutes to leech out some of the salt. After the first soak in water, soak for at least another hour in 1 cup of amaro (a digestif liqueur).

2. Roughly chop the persimmons. Simmer the chopped persimmons in $\frac{1}{2}$ cup amaro and 1 tablespoon of honey, over low heat.

3. Once the fruit is tender and the mixture is thick, remove from the heat and let cool. Once cool, stir in the rest of the amaro. Taste for sweetness and, if needed, add a drizzle more of honey. Store in a mason jar.

FRESH FIGS
PACKED IN FRESH GINGER SALT
COOKED

Yield: Approximately 2 lbs (472 ml)

INGREDIENTS

1 lb (454 g) ginger

1 cup (237 ml) mint leaves

4 cups (946 ml) sea salt

½ lb (227 g) fresh, in-season figs

Liquor of your choice, 2 cups
  [474 ml) or more, as needed

It is essential to use sweet, fresh, seasonal figs in this recipe. Yes, the purpose here is to dry the figs, but in a different way—using salt. The sweet, figgy juice in a fresh fig plays a major role in the intense sweetness and saltiness of the final product. It's not so pleasant to eat this straight-up, but it's wonderful as a condiment. Try it folded into homemade whipped cream and served over fresh, in-season strawberries and blueberries (page 180).

1. Finely mince the ginger.

2. Finely chop the mint leaves and mix the leaves and ginger into the sea salt, so that all the ingredients are uniformly distributed.

3. Mix the figs together with the ginger salt, so that the figs are well-distributed in the salt, and store in a mason jar. Allow to rest for at least one week.

TO SERVE

1. Soak the figs in water for 15 minutes to leech out the salt. Then soak for an additional 30 minutes in the liquor of your choice. Dry the figs before using them.

2. Chop or pulse the figs in a blender to create a sauce-like consistency.

PRESERVED FIG-INFUSED WHIPPED CREAM
WITH FRESH, SEASONAL BERRIES
COOKED

Yield: 4 servings

SPECIAL TOOLS
Stainless steel bowl, chilled

INGREDIENTS
1 pint (473 ml) fresh whipping
  cream
1 teaspoon (5 ml) preserved figs
  (see page 179)
1 cup (237 ml) fresh strawberries
1 cup (237 ml) fresh blueberries
2 teaspoons (10 ml) ginger salt
  (see page 179)

Folding preserved figs into fresh whipped cream achieves a yin and yang balance between the sweet and salty fig and the smooth, rich cream. Fresh strawberries and blueberries add a crunch and juiciness to the dish, perfect for a refreshing summer dessert.

1. Whip the cream until soft peaks form. A cold bowl will help the cream to stiffen.

2. Gently fold the preserved figs into the whipped cream just until incorporated.

3. Spoon the infused whipped cream over fresh, in-season strawberries and blueberries.

4. Before serving, sprinkle ginger salt over the cream.

PRESERVED SWEET MELON
SALTED AND AIR-DRIED

Yield: About 15 bite-sized pieces (depending on melon size)

SPECIAL TOOLS
Container for salting
Skewer or clips for hanging
  the melon
A line or a place to hang the
  skewer horizontally (for drying)

INGREDIENTS
One 3-lb (1.4 kg) cantaloupe
  (halved, and sliced into ½"
  [13 mm] half-circles)
5 oz (142 g) salt

When a melon is at its peak, its ripe sweetness is most intense. Coupled with the savory goodness of a great sea salt, its flavor is unparalleled. When you salt the melon and leave it to dry, what you end up with is a long-lasting, salty and sweet burst of freshness somewhere between a pickle and fruit leather.

1. Coat the melon in salt, stacking 1 piece on top of the other. Cover and let the melon rest for at least 24 hours. The salt will draw out a tremendous amount of moisture, so you'll be left with quite a brine (this brine can be used for cooking).

2. Run the skewer through the melon pieces and hang to dry in a cool, dark, breezy place for at least a week, or until dry.

FRESH FIGS PACKED IN GINGER SALT, page 179

FIG-INFUSED WHIPPED CREAM, page 180

PRESERVED LEMONS

CURED

About 10-12 lemons

SPECIAL TOOLS

Large crock or glass jar

INGREDIENTS

12 oz (340 g) sea salt

3 lbs (1.4 kg) lemons (washed
  thoroughly and quartered)

A classic in many parts of the world, preserved lemons can add dimension to a variety of dishes, including soups, stews, and roasts. They can also be used as a condiment and they can be combined with other ingredients, such as olives, capers, or pickles, to create vibrant chutneys, dipping sauces, or spreads. Preserve them in a glass jar, and they double as a beautiful kitchen décor item!

1. Pack the salt tightly into the lemons, layering salt and lemons in alternating layers, encouraging the lemons to release their juices. Make sure they are packed tightly in the jar, and weigh them down, if necessary.

2. Cover the container, making sure there is some space between the lemons and the top of the jar.

3. Let the lemons cure for at least 3 weeks.

SALTED CUCUMBERS

CURED

About 15 cucumbers

SPECIAL TOOLS

Large crock or a glass jar

A weight to keep cucumbers submerged in brine

INGREDIENTS

8 oz (227 g) salt

2 lbs (1 kg) fresh small cucumbers, washed well, with the tips removed

A little less common in the United States than vinegar pickles, salted cucumbers are a classic. No need to mix liquids and spices—salt is all that's necessary. That said, it's important to monitor your two ingredients throughout the process, as the cucumbers will go through many stages of transformation before they are fully cured. Try them on a sandwich, make a relish, or slice them thinly and arrange them on a charcuterie board.

1. Pack the salt into the cucumbers by layering the salt and cucumbers in alternating layers in a large crock. Cover with a piece of parchment paper and a weight.

2. Let the cucumbers cure for at least a week. A brine will form within two days. Make sure to stir the brine a little every day or two, to make sure the salt is evenly distributed and all the cucumbers are exposed to the brine. If there's not enough brine to cover the cucumbers, you can add a sparsely salted water solution to your crock. If the curing is going well, you'll see bubbles forming throughout the process. The cucumbers are ready to eat when there are no longer bubbles forming in the brine.

3. Store in a capped or sealed container.

SALTED BEETS

CURED

Yield: About 1½ lbs salted beets (680 g)

SPECIAL TOOLS

Nonreactive container for salting
 (I like Pyrex)
Skewer
A place to hang the skewer
 horizontally (for drying)

INGREDIENTS

2 lbs (1 kg) beets (washed
 thoroughly, stems removed, and
 sliced into ½" [13 mm] rounds)
8 oz (227 g) salt

A cross between a pickled beet and a dehydrated beet, this dish will likely attract curiosity among salt-cured vegetable enthusiasts. It can be sliced and eaten as is, with a good piece of bread and the right condiment.

1. In a nonreactive container, coat the beets in salt and let them rest for at least 24 hours.

2. Skewer the beets and hang them horizontally in a cool, dark, breezy place for at least 1 week, or until sufficiently dry.

3. If they're too salty, purge them in cold water and pat dry before eating.

SALTED TANGERINES
CURED

Yield: About 9 tangerines

SPECIAL TOOLS
Large glass jar or crock
A weight to keep tangerines
submerged in brine

INGREDIENTS
4 oz (113 g) sea salt
1 lb (454 g) tangerines, washed
thoroughly and quartered
1 mini-chili pepper (I like Thai
chilis), washed and sliced thinly

Salted tangerines are nice to use in cooking, as a food condiment, or as a base for a pungent chutney or salsa. One way I like to use them is in a mostarda (see page 188). Another thought is to incorporate them into an ice cream. If stored properly, these will last a long time.

1. Pack the salt tightly into the tangerines by building alternating layers of salt and tangerine. Distribute the chili pepper slices evenly throughout the cure.

2. Cover with a piece of parchment paper and a weight. A brine will form within a day or so.

3. Loosely cover the container and let the tangerines ferment for at least 1 week.

4. Once fermentation is complete, tighten the cover and store in a cool place. You can store these in their brine.

MOSTARDA
WITH SALTED TANGERINES AND FIGS
COOKED

Yield: About 1½ cups (355 ml)

INGREDIENTS

1 cup (237) red wine

½ cup (118 ml) grappa

½ cup (118 ml) cane sugar

⅓ cup (78 ml) mustard seeds

½ cup (118 ml) salted tangerines
 (see page 187), diced

½ cup (118 ml) dry figs, diced

½ cup (118 ml) Dijon mustard

Mostarda is one of the world's great condiments. It is an amalgamation of two powerful flavors that are rarely found in the same bite: sweet and pungent. The sweetness arouses a sense of cheerfulness on the tongue, while pungency provides a sharp clarity. Try the mostarda with meat, fish, or cheese, or simply spread it atop some warm bread.

1. Combine the wine, grappa, and sugar in a saucepan and bring to a boil.

2. Reduce to a simmer and let simmer for 10 minutes.

3. Add the mustard seeds and simmer another 3 or 4 minutes.

4. Stir in the tangerines, figs, and mustard, stirring well to combine, and remove from heat.

5. Let cool and store in a glass jar.

6. Finish with an additional (small) splash of grappa, if desired.

7. Wait at least 1 hour before serving, so the fruit can soak up the liquid.

MOSTARDA

FLAKY BREAKFAST PASTRY
WITH SALTED TANGERINES AND FARMER CHEESE
COOKED

Yield: 8 servings

INGREDIENTS

20 salted tangerine rounds
(see page 187)

About 2 cups [473 ml] rum, or
enough to cover the tangerine
rounds

Flaky tart crust with leaf lard
(see page 63)

8 oz (227 g) farmer cheese

¼ cup (59 ml) cane sugar
(for sprinkling on top of pastry)

This recipe is a variation on the classic Cuban pastry, called "Pastelito de Guayaba y Queso." It is traditionally eaten for breakfast or as an afternoon snack with coffee. If made correctly, the crust is perfectly flaky. It can be prepared quickly, especially if you make the crust ahead of time.

1. Preheat oven to 425°F (218°C).

2. Soak tangerine rounds in water for half an hour to leech out the salt. Soak again in rum, for 1 hour or overnight.

3. Roll out the tart crust to a ½" (13 mm) thickness, and cut two 8" x 10" (20 cm x 25.5 cm) rectangles of dough.

4. Place 1 sheet of pastry dough on a greased baking sheet. Cover with a layer of farmer cheese. Layer tangerine rounds over the cheese, and top with the second layer of pastry. Sprinkle some cane sugar on top.

5. Place the baking sheet in the oven, lower the oven temperature to 400°F (204°C), and bake for approximately 20 minutes, or until golden brown.

6. Cut into squares and serve with coffee.

PRESERVED MUSHROOMS
SALTED AND AIR-DRIED
CURED

Yield: About 10 oz (283 g)

SPECIAL TOOLS

A line for drying

Twine

INGREDIENTS

1 cup (237 ml) sea salt

¼ cup (59 ml) water

1 lb (454 g) fresh, in-season
chanterelles (or wild mushrooms
of your choice)

Creating salted, air-dried mushrooms is a beautiful way to preserve seasonal mushroom harvests for the off-season. They're a little different from other dry-cured vegetables, as they're meant for cooking, not eating. What you'll end up with is a transformed version of the original mushroom—one that is a little bit rubbery, quite dry, and very salty, but no less interesting and useful in the kitchen. Once dry, they'll last quite some time—at least a couple of months.

1. In a crock or a wide-mouthed mason jar, dissolve 1 tablespoon (15 ml) of salt in ¼ cup (59 ml) of water.

2. Add chanterelles to the container and gently shake until the chanterelles are slightly moist (this will help the salt to stick).

3. Add the rest of the salt and coat the mushrooms until the salt is evenly distributed.

4. Leave the chanterelles in the salt for 12 hours, gently shaking the container at least 3 times during the 12 hours to make sure the salt is well-distributed.

5. After 12 hours, remove the chanterelles from the salt. Quickly and gently rinse off all salt.

6. With twine, tie a knot around each of the chanterelle stems, creating a "string of chanterelles," with a loop on each end of the twine for hanging. Make sure that the chanterelles are close together, but not touching each other. Hang in a cool, airy place for at least 1 week or until well-dried.

7. Once dry, store the chanterelles in an airtight container or a vacuum pouch. Before using them, rehydrate them in water or another liquid for at least half an hour.

LEAF LARD AND BUTTERMILK BISCUITS

LEAF LARD AND BUTTERMILK BISCUITS
COOKED

Yield: About 8 biscuits

SPECIAL TOOLS
Pastry cutter
Biscuit cutter
  (or a drinking glass)

INGREDIENTS
4 cups (946 ml) all-purpose flour
2 tablespoons (30 ml) pure cane
  sugar
2 tablespoons (30 ml) baking
  powder
1 teaspoon (5 ml) salt
14 oz (397 g) leaf lard, chilled
  and cubed
2 cups (473 ml) whole milk

WINE PAIRING

Pair with an unoaked crisp white,
such as Chardonnay or Chenin
Blanc.

Oh, biscuits—biscuits and the warm memories they conjure up—of lazy weekend days, snowed-in school days, gatherings of loved ones, or road-trip sandwiches. In short, biscuits usually make things better. Here is a recipe for "quick" biscuits, made with leaf lard, arguably the most incredible baking fat on earth. Among the many wonderful things about biscuits is how versatile they are. They can be sweet, savory, or in between. Using the following recipe, you can add things like cheese, cured meats, and fresh herbs, to name just a few, to create something savory and delicious. Conversely, chocolate, berries, or candied nuts can be added to give you something sweet and decadent.

1. Mix together the flour, sugar, baking powder, and salt.

2. Cut in the leaf lard using a pastry cutter (this can also be done using a food processor with a few touches of the "pulse" function) until the mixture is the consistency of coarse sand.

3. Create a well in the middle of your dough and slowly add the milk, giving the mixture two swift stirs while adding the milk to ensure that it is getting evenly incorporated. Make sure not to overwork the dough, as the more you work this mixture, the tougher your biscuits will be.

4. Place the dough in a bowl, and allow it to rest in the refrigerator for at least half an hour. While the mixture is resting, preheat the oven to 450°F (232°C) and grease a baking sheet.

5. Remove the mixture and, on a floured surface, shape the dough into a rectangle about 1" (2.5 cm) thick, using your hands. Take care to handle the mixture as little as possible. Use extra flour as needed in this step to make sure the dough has structural integrity and doesn't stick to the surface.

6. With a biscuit cutter or a drinking glass, cut into the biscuit dough, using just enough flour to keep the biscuits from sticking to the cutter. Place the biscuits on a greased baking sheet.

7. Put the biscuits in the oven and lower the temperature to 425°F (218°C). Bake until risen and golden brown. Check after 10 minutes.

YEASTED BISCUITS
WITH LEAF LARD
COOKED

Yield: Approximately 8 biscuits

SPECIAL TOOLS
Pastry cutter
Biscuit cutter (or drinking glass)

INGREDIENTS
½ cup (118 ml) lukewarm water

4 tablespoons (60 ml) pure cane sugar

1 packet active, dry yeast (or 2/3 oz [19 g] cake yeast)

4 cups (946 ml) all-purpose flour

2 tablespoons (30 ml) baking powder

1 tablespoon (15 ml) salt

14 oz (397 g) leaf lard (chilled and cubed)

1 ½ cups (355 ml) whole milk

WINE PAIRING

Pair with an unoaked crisp white, such as Chardonnay or Chenin Blanc.

These may not seem a whole lot different from the Leaf Lard and Buttermilk Biscuits on page 193, but their layered flakiness, sheet-like inner composition, and gentle fermented taste will prove they are indeed in a league of their own. This cross between biscuits and yeast rolls is also known as "Angel Biscuits" or "Bride Biscuits." In my opinion, if a blissful start to a day were a biscuit, it would be baked with this recipe, regardless of what you call them. As with the Leaf Lard and Buttermilk Biscuits, you can go savory or sweet here. One of my favorite additions is dry chorizo and a good clothbound cheddar.

1. Preheat oven to 450°F (232°C).

2. Activate the yeast by mixing ½ cup (118 ml) lukewarm water with 2 tablespoons (30 ml) sugar, dissolving the sugar well, then adding the dry yeast. Let the yeast "wake up" for about 15 minutes (you'll know it's ready when it starts to bubble; if it doesn't, your yeast is no good). Set aside.

3. Combine flour, 2 tablespoons (30 ml) sugar, baking powder, and salt. Cut in the leaf lard using a pastry cutter (this can also be done using a food processor with the "pulse" function) until the mixture is the consistency of coarse sand.

4. Create a well in the middle of your dough and slowly add the yeast mixture, then the milk, giving the liquids a few swift stirs to ensure that everything is evenly incorporated.

5. Knead the dough with 10–15 strokes. The idea is to knead just enough to agitate the gluten, but not so much that your biscuits will be tough. About 12 strokes should do it.

6. Place the dough in a bowl and cover at room temperature for 1 hour. (This can also be done overnight in the refrigerator.)

7. After the dough has rested, roll the dough out to 1" (2.5 cm) thick.

8. Using a biscuit cutter or a drinking glass, cut into biscuits, using as little flour as needed to keep the biscuits from sticking to the cutter. Place the biscuits on a greased baking sheet.

9. Put the biscuits in the oven and lower the oven temperature to 425°F (218°C). Bake until the biscuits are risen and golden brown (about 10 minutes or so).

CHICORY SALAD
WITH LENTILS, SEARED ROOT VEGETABLES, SHEEP MILK CHEESE, THINLY SLICED SALAMI, AND PORK CRACKLINS

COOKED

Yield: 2 servings

INGREDIENTS

For Salad

½ cup (118 ml) French green lentils

Salt to taste

2 carrots—cut in half and quartered lengthwise to create 8 spears

2 parsnips—cut in half and quartered lengthwise (or 8 baby parsnips)

2 golden beets (cut into cubes)

1 bunch washed, dried, and roughly chopped chicory

For Vinaigrette

½ teaspoon (2.5 ml) whole-grain mustard

1 tablespoon (15 ml) fresh lemon juice

3 tablespoons (45 ml) olive oil

For Topping

¾ cup (177 ml) warm, fresh pork cracklins (left over from making lard) or bacon, cut into 1" (2.5 cm) pieces, and fried until crispy

¼ lb (114 g) well-aged sheep milk cheese, thinly shaved

I love fresh chicory for its earthy, tender, and slightly bitter nature. You might think it's a bit off the beaten path, but it is actually widely available. It lends itself really well to warm salads, in which you give some of the elements of the salad a quick cooking, as is shown here. You can also substitute the fresh root vegetables here with various cured vegetable recipes from earlier on. If you don't have cracklins handy, use crispy bacon instead.

1. Boil the lentils in salted water. Drain and set aside.

2. Blanch the carrots, parsnips, and beets in salted, boiling water. Drain and sauté briefly in a very hot skillet, with a little olive oil. Set aside.

3. Make the vinaigrette by combining the mustard and lemon juice, then stirring in the olive oil.

4. Separately, toss the chicory and lentils, then the root vegetables in the vinaigrette, coating them lightly.

5. Serve by plating the chicory/lentils first, then the root vegetables arranged on top, and finish with the cracklins and the shaved cheese.

WINE PAIRING

Pair with a full-bodied red, like Cabernet Sauvignon or Petit Syrah.

APRICOT BRUSCHETTA
WITH SALTED CHANTERELLES AND FARMER CHEESE
COOKED

Yield: 3 bruschetta

SPECIAL TOOLS

Pastry cutter

Biscuit cutter (or drinking glass)

INGREDIENTS

5 oz (142 g) salted, air dried
   mushrooms, coarsely chopped

2 cups (473 ml) port wine

A dash of olive oil for sautéing
   (approximately 1 tablespoon [15 ml])

5 oz (142 g) fresh farmer cheese,
   cubed

5 oz (142 g) dry apricot salami
   (removed from casing)

3 thick slices crusty peasant bread

Salt to taste (approximately
   ½ teaspoon [2.5 ml])

A few sprigs thyme, stems
   removed and chopped

A squeeze of lemon

Bruschetta can be made in a short period of time with either fresh or day-old bread. It can be a snack, an appetizer, or a whole meal. What I love about this particular bruschetta is the marriage of its contrasting flavors. You have three major taste bud senses at work here—salty, umami, and sweet—along with a nice amalgamation of textures. The pungency of the mushrooms, the mildness of the cheese, and the relative intensity of the apricots come together in a manner that highlights how effective stark flavor contrasts can be.

1. Soak the mushrooms in the port for at least 30 minutes.

2. Just before the mushrooms have finished soaking, place a sauté pan over a high flame.

3. Drain the mushrooms, reserving the liquid, and sauté them in the very hot sauté pan for 2 minutes with a little olive oil. Set aside.

4. In a separate pan, reduce the port over a medium-low flame until it has reached a sauce-like consistency, similar to the thickness of mango nectar.

5. Toss the mushrooms and cheese together with salt and 1 tablespoon (15 ml) reduced port.

6. Smear the apricot "salami" on the bread. Top with the mushrooms and cheese, and warm in the oven, if desired.

7. Finish with chopped thyme and a small squeeze of lemon.

HANGOVER-CURING GRILLED CHEESE

COOKED

Yield: 1 sandwich

SPECIAL TOOLS

Cast-iron skillet

A press (could be a common
  bacon press, a brick wrapped in
  aluminum foil, or another heavy
  skillet)

INGREDIENTS

1 onion, sliced into strips

2 tablespoons (30 ml) compound
  lard (see recipe on page 65) (Plain
  lard or bacon fat will also work. If
  you don't have either, substitute
  3 tablespoons [45 ml] olive oil or
  butter.)

1 tablespoon (15 ml) maple syrup

2 oz (57 g) clothbound cheddar

2 oz (57 g) gruyère

1 tablespoon (15 ml) whole-grain
  mustard

2 thick slices of peasant bread

3 thin slices prosciutto

6 thin slices lomo embuchado

4 thin slices bresaola

2 thin slices lardo

5 slices pickles

Fresh herbs of your choice,
  chopped

This "kitchen sink" approach to grilled cheese is full of flavor, body, and energy. It's great for a hangover, when something comforting is all you need, or as a sobering, nap-inducing lunch.

1. Caramelize the onions by sautéing them in compound lard on medium-high heat until they are well-coated and begin to soften. Add maple syrup and reduce heat, stirring occasionally, until the onions are tender and caramelized.

2. Grate the cheese.

3. Spread the mustard on the bread and layer the meat on the bread with a heap of caramelized onions, followed by the cheese, herbs, and pickles.

4. Heat a little dollop of lard in the skillet and press. Grill the sandwich until the cheese is melted and the bread is crunchy and browning. Slice in half on a bias.

5. *Optional:* To round out the plate, serve with French Fries in Lard (see page 64).

HANGOVER-CURING GRILLED CHEESE, page 197

CHICORY SALAD, page 195

INDEX

1 Dry-Cured Whole Leg of Pork 2 Truffle Salami 3 Salami Picante 4 Mojama
5 Fig "Salami" 6 Large Country Salami 7 Picante 8 Beer Salami 9 Beer Salami (Small)
10 Beer Salami (Large) 11 Pepperoni 12 Salami Picante (Small) 13 Country Salami
14 Large Chorizo 15 Bresaola

ACKNOWLEDGMENTS

Special thank you to my wife, my father, my mother, Alba, and my sister. I could not do this without you. Thank you for all the love and support.

To my father, for being the valiant mentor and foundation for my values and my ambition. You are truly a treasure to the universe, and I thank you for being the example of humanity that you have been.

To my wife: Thank you for your love, support, companionship, partnership, encouragement, and belief in me; for being there for me and patiently forgoing months' worth of weekends so that I may finish this book; for loving me.

To my mother, for never giving up on me and always wanting better for me, and for giving me the encouragement to pursue a field that I believe in when most of the family had a hard time making sense of what I was doing.

To Alba: Thank you for possessing the most patient and optimistic spirit I have ever known. You have been there for me every step of the way and I am eternally grateful for the impact you have made on my life.

Gracias por poseer esa gran paciencia y espíritu optimista que nunca había visto. Siempre has estado dispuesta a ayudarme en todos los momentos y estaré eternamente agradecido por el impacto que has causado en mi vida.

To my sister: Thank you for being such a loving and supportive sibling. Your heart is gold and your compassion is infinite. I couldn't ask for a better sister. Thank you.

Charles Wekselbaum was born and raised in New York City in a Cuban-Jewish-American household. Food, the tools used to prepare it, and the importance of cooking from scratch were always central elements in his family's household. He considers himself very fortunate to have grown up in such a food-centric household, in such a multi-cultural city. This immersion in the foods of his family, and the foods of the diverse cultures that surrounded him growing up, helped form the groundwork for what has emerged as the centerpiece of his working life as an adult, Charlito's Cocina, producer of hand-crafted charcuterie and more.

Charles began Charlito's Cocina in 2010 at a personal and professional crossroads in his life, with a simple two-fold mission: First, to make delicious foods, cured in traditional manners, from the cleanest, best ingredients he could find. Second, to figure out how to make these foods affordable, approachable, and accessible to a wider audience, to help restore integrity and trust in a food system that has, for a variety of complex reasons, instilled reservation and doubt in many of the very people whom it is intended to serve.

Charlito's Cocina is now a thriving producer of delicious cured meats. It has come a long way from its first 25-pound batch of sellable salami to producing thousands of pounds per month, with an audience that spans nearly all 50 states. It supplies traditionally made dry-cured salamis, as well as other hand-crafted charcuterie to chefs, small independent grocery stores, and larger scale markets around the country.

Charles believes wholeheartedly in working tirelessly, but also in stepping back from work when need be, which is essential to doing a job well. When he is not working, he likes to spend time with his family, listen to the blues, ride a bike, and try to smell the roses.